A Guide to The General Assembly of the Church of Scotland

New Edition

ANDREW HERRON

THE SAINT ANDREW PRESS
EDINBURGH

First published in 1976 by
THE SAINT ANDREW PRESS
121 George Street, Edinburgh

ISBN 0 7152 0595 1

This edition 1986

British Library Cataloging in Publication Data
Herron, Andrew
A Guide to the General Assembly of the Church of Scotland.–New ed.
1. Church of Scotland, *General Assembly*
I. Title
262′.552411 BX9078

ISBN 0–7152–0595–1

Printed and bound in Great Britain by
Bell and Bain Limited, Glasgow.

Contents

Foreword

by Brigadier Lord Ballantrae,
KT, GCMG, GCVO, DSO, OBE

Lord High Commissioner
1973 and 1974

'The procedures and machinery of the General Assembly are antiquated, cumbersome, incomprehensible, and–in two, plain, old, Scots words–"clean gyte".'

How often has one heard this said or something like it; and could any of us swear on oath that he has never said it himself? Most people who have served a term or two as Commissioners can remember occasions when the Assembly have got themselves into a proper fankle; when nine-tenths of the Commissioners cannot for the life of them make out whether they are voting on a Motion, a Counter-Motion, an Amendment, or an Amendment to an Amendment. They have witnessed three-cornered arguments, always good-tempered and sometimes hilarious, between the Leader of the House, the Principal Clerk and the august Moderator himself, as to where on earth–or elsewhere–the Venerable Assembly have got to.

The older of us remember with affectionate relish the salty fashion in which the late and incomparable Dr MacNicol of Longforgan used to unravel us. Later on, it was Dr Longmuir of Chirnside who dug us sardonically out of the procedural snowdrifts in which we had got stuck; Jim Longmuir, whose early death deprived the Kirk of one of the sagest men who ever served it.

But in fact the procedures and machinery are far from daft or cumbersome if one masters them. They derive from centuries of experience, and were evolved by men who knew what they were about. The difficulty is that there has hitherto been no simple guide to them, so that they remain undeniably bewildering to people encountering them for the first time. Such people may well return to their home parishes at the end of the ten days as confused as they were at the beginning; and small blame to them. The first time that I attended the Assembly as a Commissioner, in 1956 or thereabouts, I didn't (so to speak) know my glengarry from my spats.

This short book by Dr Herron is therefore long overdue, and nobody has better qualifications than he to be its author. He has already demonstrated the power and pith of his pen in other writings, including a notable book; he has been Parish Minister, Clerk to the Presbytery of Glasgow, Leader of the House and Moderator, and is a qualified lawyer forbye. The book is all sinew, with no superfluous flesh, easy to read, and interesting in its own right. Having once read it, nobody need ever feel bewildered again.

I commend this book not only to all Commissioners of Assembly, but to all members of the Church of Scotland: because there is much ignorance about how the Assembly functions, and what it is all about. I am not ashamed to confess that the reading of it in typescript has explained to me much about which I was vague, or even ignorant, before. We should have had something like it in our hands years ago, and we are deep in Dr Herron's debt that we have it now.

Preface

He must be a strange person indeed who can come away from his first Assembly without having been profoundly impressed. How often have I heard Elders (from remote country district and busy city alike) tell of how at the Assembly they have gained a new picture of the Kirk to which they belong. I have a conviction, however, that the value of their first attendance would be enhanced had they better understanding of the mechanics of the whole affair; if, at the lowest estimate, they were better able to find their way about–through the premises themselves, through the labyrinth of documents that come into their hands, and through the intricate maze of debate.

This booklet is directed primarily at the person-in-the-pew (referred to in days of unregenerate male chauvinism as the man-in-the-pew), but it has also, I feel confident, much to say to the average parson-in-the-pulpit, and the most hardened Assembly-goer should find something of interest in its pages–even if it is only something with which to disagree.

The intensely interesting thing about each Assembly is, of course, what might be called its 'personality', the qualities that mark it out as different from every other Assembly. But that is something that has got to be experienced and about which nothing can be written in advance. Whatever may be the individual character of any one Assembly it will still be run on the same lines, with the same Standing Orders, following the identical general pattern, as all others. It is that general pattern that I have here tried to explain.

For I believe that an understanding of that pattern can enable the Commissioner–even at his first Assembly–not just to be impressed by it but to understand it, to appreciate it, and, in the fullest sense, to enjoy it.

I am deeply indebted to Lord Ballantrae for the typically generous Foreword which he so readily undertook to provide–and that for two reasons. First, I know of no-one who has a more intimate understanding of the Assembly and its peculiar ways or a deeper love for it. Second, it was he who in the first place suggested that I should try to produce such a booklet.

Glasgow, 1976 ANDREW HERRON

Preface to the New Edition

Since this little Guide was produced ten years ago a great deal of water has flowed under the bridges, a great many copies have passed through the bookshops, and a great many changes have overtaken the General Assembly.

It is the last consideration which has inspired the production of this new edition. A map produced before the motorways is not of much use to the motorist of today, and a Guide to the General Assembly that is going to direct and not to mislead has got to be up-to-date.

Since the book was having to be reprinted, occasion was taken not merely to amend and up-date the material but in effect to rewrite the whole affair. We have adhered to the original pattern and have reproduced some parts nearly verbatim, but we have made at least two major additions. First there is a 'run-down' on the new Committee structure, this being an attempt to indicate in very brief compass the field covered by each of the Committees and to show how they are grouped into Boards and Departments. Second there is a series of 'Notes' covering matters which intimately affect the business of the court, and this is an attempt to look at these in somewhat greater depth than was possible when the subject in question initially arose in the course of the narrative.

While, then, this booklet still has the same objective of making the Assembly and its business more easily comprehensible to the first-timer, it is designed also to take its place alongside the other two Guides by providing material of interest and value to the more experienced Assembly-goer.

It is our hope that the booklet may have some success in achieving both of these objectives.

Glasgow, 1986 ANDREW HERRON

1

The Time, The Place, and the People

If you are properly to understand–not to say enjoy–your first experience as a Commissioner to the General Assembly, it is essential you should know one or two simple facts about the mechanics of the whole affair: where they meet, when they meet, who are the officials, how to find your way around the premises, and so on. This opening chapter is designed to answer some of these simple questions.

Meetings and Services

Place of Meeting–For a very long time now the General Assembly have met in Edinburgh, although there is no constitutional reason why they should meet there–indeed two of the most famous Assemblies of all time were those that met at Perth in 1618 and at Glasgow twenty years later. But that was a long time ago. It is very convenient today to meet in Edinburgh, so there, I imagine, they will stay. Since 1929 the meetings have invariably been held in the Assembly Hall on the Mound.

Time of Meeting–Since 1978 the Assembly have convened on a Saturday morning around the middle of May, continuing until the evening of the following Friday when they conclude with a session, public in character, at which various groups of people are presented (*p* 23).

Assembly Service—This takes place in the High Kirk (St Giles' Cathedral) at 11.00 on the Sunday morning and is attended by the Lord High Commissioner and his suite. Normally the service is conducted by the Moderator who also preaches. In the course of the afternoon a Gaelic Service is held in Greyfriars Tolbooth and Highland Church in Greyfriars Place.

Sunday Evening—A sederunt of the Assembly convenes in the Hall at 6.30 on the Sunday evening (*p* 22).

Holy Communion—The Sacrament is celebrated in the Assembly Hall immediately before the beginning of Monday's business sederunt, that is, at 9.30 am (*p* 22).

Garden Party—This is given by the Lord High Commissioner and is held in the grounds of the Palace of Holyroodhouse at 3.30 in the afternoon of the opening day (Saturday), and to this Commissioners and their spouses are invited (*p* 79).

Members

The numerical strength of the Assembly varies slightly from one year to the next, generally downward as the number of parishes shrinks, although it has recently levelled out at just over the 1300 mark. In 1985 it was 1318, made up of 1250 Commissioners, 6 Members *ex-Officiis*, 32 Corresponding Members and 30 Delegates. There were also 12 Visitors (not included in the total). It is well to understand the distinctions which these terms represent.

Commissioners—These are ministers and elders appointed in equal numbers by Presbyteries. It is important to note that they are Commissioners and not–as is sometimes supposed–delegates. They cannot be instructed how they are to vote on any issue. What their commission requires is that they 'repair thereto, attend all the diets of the same, and there consult, vote and determine in all matters that come before them to the glory of God and the good of His Church, according to the Word of God and the Confession of Faith, and agreeable to the constitution of this Church, as they will be answerable'. Each Presbytery is entitled to appoint ministers and elders in the proportion of one for every four or part of four on the Presbytery Roll at the end of the calendar year. In order to qualify for a commission an elder has to be a *bona fide* acting elder, that is to say, he has to be a 'live' member of a Kirk Session. He does not need to be a member of Presbytery.

Members ex-Officiis–These are six in number: the Moderator, the Moderator Designate, the two Clerks, the Procurator, and the Solicitor of the Church. It was in 1956 that these office-bearers became members (full members enjoying all the rights and privileges of Commissioners) in virtue of their offices. Prior to that each one had to receive a commission from a Presbytery in the normal way.

Corresponding Members–These are of two classes: first, Missionaries and Chaplains (ministers or elders) who are at home on ordinary leave; and second, representatives of certain Standing Committees who are allowed to attend with a view to watching over the interests of their Committees. The President of the Woman's Guild and the Editor of *Life and Work* are also allowed to sit in this capacity. Corresponding Members are entitled to attend all sessions of the Assembly and to speak thereat, but they have no voting rights (and therefore no right to propose a motion).

Delegates–These are members of other denominations, with which the Church of Scotland has close ties, appointed by the appropriate body within their own communion. Their status is exactly the same as that of Corresponding Members (see above) except that they are specifically barred from taking any part in judicial matters.

Visitors–The Assembly is attended also by a limited number of visitors generally from overseas, accredited by their own Churches, but with no official position and with no rights of voting or even of speaking. Since 1969 the Roman Catholic hierarchy in Scotland has been invited to send a representative. He is designed as an 'Invited Visitor' but his official status is simply that of a Visitor.

Officials

The Moderator–Like every other court in the Church, the General Assembly are presided over by a Moderator. He is elected by the Assembly at the start of the first day's proceedings. He has been nominated in the previous October by a committee consisting of the seven immediately past surviving Moderators, seven elders elected by the Assembly, and 47 persons appointed by Presbyteries. It is his business to preside, to keep good order, to rule on points of order, to refuse to accept motions that are offensive, irrelevant or otherwise incompetent, and to sign documents on behalf of the Assembly. He has a casting but not a deliberative vote. (See Note re 'Moderator', *p* 82).

When it is not convenient for the Moderator to preside in person at any part of a sederunt he arranges for one or other of his predecessors to act in his stead.

In 1973 the Baird Trustees celebrated the centenary of their foundation. During those hundred years the Trust had done much to further the work of the Church of

Scotland, not least in helping to provide and maintain buildings, and to mark the occasion the Trustees made the offer that they would provide and endow a house where the Moderator with his Chaplains could reside during the Assembly (they had had to resort to a hotel up to this point). In conjuction with the National Trust for Scotland the two upper floors of the Georgian House at 7 Charlotte Square were purchased, renovated, furnished and endowed to provide such a residence, and this nowadays the Moderator generally uses as his base throughout his year in office.

Moderator's Chaplains—The Moderator is attended by a Senior and a Junior Chaplain, who assist him in the organising and arranging of the wide variety of matters that fall within his care, having a particular responsibility for the social aspects of his duty. They wear full ministerial robes and follow the Moderator in his procession.

The Clerks—There is a Principal Clerk and a Depute Clerk who between them have the duty of keeping the record of the proceedings and who are on hand to advise the Moderator if need arises on matters of procedure. The Principal Clerk occupies the central chair below the Moderator and the Depute Clerk sits on his right.

There is a Clerks' Office on the mezzanine floor above the Common Room where someone is always in attendance, and it is here that Notices of Motion should be given in and any messages for the Clerks should be left.

The Procurator—The Procurator is a Queen's Counsel appointed by the Assembly. In the wig, gown and bands appropriate to his status he sits on the left of the Principal Clerk. Constitutionally it is his duty to advise on matters before the Assembly on which the law of the land has a particular bearing, but in addition to this the Procurator may (at the request of the Moderator and not on a demand from the floor) advise the Assembly on any matter that is before the court–generally, of course, on its legal or procedural aspects. He offers advice–the Assembly are liable to get very cross if this is referred to as 'giving a ruling'.

Business Convener–One of the first things to be done by each Assembly is to appoint a Business Committee to supervise the daily order of proceedings (prepared in advance by the Board of Practice and Procedure) and generally to ensure that the arrangements for the various sederunts are orderly managed. The Convener is frequently referred to as 'the leader of the house' (although normally the Assembly indignantly refuse to be called a 'house'). He sits at the table in front of the Clerks and on the Moderator's right, and is expected to give guidance on the conduct of the business, on the method of taking the vote, and on questions of order, to take things in a firm hand when some procedural crisis arises, and generally to be available to advise the Moderator on request.

The Vice-Convener of the Business Committee is to be found at the same table, opposite his Convener to whom he acts as deputy and assistant in the 'leading of the house'.

It is interesting that these two gentlemen are generally the only two commissioners still to be seen in clerical frock-coats. Not so long ago every Convener giving in a report was so attired. And not so long before that every commissioner!

Solicitor of the Church–The legal affairs of the pre-Union Church of Scotland were in the hands of the Solicitor, the Free Church had its Custodier of Titles, and the United Presbyterian Church employed a Law Agent. The three offices have now been united into one, and the holder of the office is usually referred to as the Solicitor of the

Church. He sits at the table opposite the Business Convener and his principal part in the affairs of the Assembly has to do with property transactions.

Precentor—For those with roots in the Scottish Kirk this officer needs no explanation. For others it is sufficient to say that he 'gives the note' for the opening praise at each sederunt.

Officer—In common with other courts the General Assembly appoint an Officer to wait upon their proceedings and to execute their orders. In practical terms the principal function of the Officer is to be in charge of processions, to call for order before the day's sederunt begins and, where appropriate, to be of service to the Moderator's Chaplains. He also looks after the catering arrangements for the Moderator's lunch parties.

Stewards—There are a number of stewards constantly on duty throughout the hall, checking tickets at the various doors, taking charge of the issue of official papers and looking after the cloakroom. They are always ready to be helpful to anyone seeking information or advice.

Ex-Moderators—It must be emphasised that these are not 'officials' in any sense, even though the front bench on the Moderator's left is reserved for their use and even though they parade in full dress at the opening and closing sessions. They are Commissioners like any others–although not quite. For, since 1969, Presbyteries have been empowered if they so desire to return as Commissioners ex-Moderators who are members of their court in addition to the number to which they are otherwise entitled; and if they do this they send also an additional elder or elders.

Shorthand Writer—Time was when a verbatim record of each Assembly was duly printed and circulated afterwards to Commissioners–the volume could run to 800 pages of small type. The war years saw the end of that practice. A verbatim account is still kept, however, in typescript and is available for references at at any time in the Clerk's Room in the Church Offices. A young lady may be seen flitting around the Hall during debates alighting for a moment beside a recent speaker. She is the shorthand writer's assistant and is checking on the identity of those who have contributed to the debate.

The Lord High Commissioner

This is probably as good a point as any at which to say a word about the dignitary known as the Lord High Commissioner, although he must not be regarded as in any sense an official of the Assembly–both the Commissioner and the Assembly would violently (and properly) resist any such suggestion.

The roots of the office of the Queen's Commissioner lie very close to those of the Reformed Kirk in Scotland. From the earliest days of General Assemblies it was obvious that a vital question affecting the legality of their meetings and the validity of their proceedings, not to say the effectiveness of their judgments, was the question of how far they met under the Royal Assent. At one time the Crown claimed the right to say when and where Assemblies were to meet–otherwise they would not be constitutional gatherings. This, naturally, was bitterly contested. At the same time the Kirk could not object if the King wanted to know what the Assemblies were up to. So long as the royal interest did not amount to royal interference the Kirk had no ground for complaint. As a compromise the custom was established whereby a Commissioner was appointed by the Crown, but since each side had a different idea of the purpose of his presence and of the extent of his powers there was clearly room for trouble.

It was during the reign of King Charles I that things came to a head, and it happened at the famous Glasgow Assembly of 1638. The King's Commissioner of that year, the Marquis of Hamilton, when he had failed to prevent the bishops being put on trial, solemnly in the name of the King dissolved the Assembly and himself withdrew. He was followed by two ministers and three elders; the other 235 sat on and wrote what was to prove the first chapter of a long sad story of bitterness and persecution.

The Revolution Settlement of 1693, however, finally resolved the question of 'the intrinsic power of the Church' and it did so in the Church's favour, and this was fully ratified when the Treaty of Union of 1707 secured for the people of Scotland in all succeeding generations the Protestant religion and Presbyterian Church government. From that day to this each monarch on accession to the throne swears to uphold that position.

Today, as much as before, the Lord High Commissioner is appointed by the Queen to supply her own Royal Presence; he is housed in the Palace of Holyroodhouse; in the matter of precedence he follows immediately behind the Duke of Edinburgh and the Duke of Rothesay (better known perhaps as the Prince of Wales) and before the other members of the Royal Family; the royal banner in Scotland, the lion rampant, is flown over the Palace during the period of his residence; he is referred to as 'Lord' and addressed as 'Your Grace'. But he is not a member of Assembly; he sits in a gallery apart; and he addresses the court only when invited to do so. Instead of dissolving one Assembly and appointing the next (as the Stuart kings so passionately wanted to do) he undertakes to report to Her Majesty that the Assembly have concluded their business and have appointed the date of their next meeting.

The Purse-Bearer–Always in attendance upon the Lord High Commissioner is an officer known as the Purse-Bearer: as a symbol of his office he carries over his left arm a magnificently embroidered velvet 'purse'. (I have often been intrigued to wonder how much coin of the realm it contains!) While Lord High Commissioners come and go (they are usually appointed for two successive years) the Purse-Bearer continues in office and is responsible for all the behind-the-scenes organisation that is so necessary if the party at the Palace are to fulfil their desperately busy schedule of public engagements. He has an Office and a modest staff based at the Palace.

The Shakers–Each morning as he arrives the Lord High Commissioner is met at the archway entering the Quadrangle by a company of two ministers and an elder who shake him by the hand and in the name of the Assembly welcome him and his party. They then fall in to his procession and a place is found for them in his gallery. They have, presumably, a correct designation–I have myself never heard them called anything but 'the shakers'.

The Premises

Very shortly after the Disruption of 1843 the Free Church built a college for the training of its ministers. This, which was called New College, was situated on the Mound and now forms part of the University of Edinburgh. Within the college complex they incorporated an Assembly Hall. The site, which was once occupied by the residence of Mary of Guise, runs right through from the Mound to the Lawnmarket. Within recent years responsibility for the college buildings has passed from the Church to the University, but the Assembly Hall with some ancillary accommodation remains the property of the Church, and at the time of the transfer provision was made whereby at Assembly season some of what are normally college rooms are made available for Assembly business.

A rough idea of the geography of these premises is of great value–particularly to the newcomer. So let us go on a tour.

The Quadrangle – Entering from the Mound the member passes through an archway and finds himself in the Quadrangle. In front of him (or her) is a massive flight of steps while on his left there stands the statue of John Knox. The great Reformer is buried in the old graveyard to the south of St Giles' Cathedral at a spot once marked by a small metal plate inset in the roadway and inscribed 'I K 1572'. A very select few are allowed to park their cars in the Quadrangle.

The Black-and-White Corridor – Having climbed the stairs and passed through the doorway the member finds himself in the Black-and-White Corridor, a most impressive passage-way, lined with portraits, running at right-angles to his line of entry, and taking its name from the tiles with which the floor is laid. Immediately facing him as he comes into the corridor is an oak double-door (possibly flanked by a couple of lads from the BB) leading to the Lord High Commissioner's Gallery. On either side of this central doorway are situated doors which lead through into the Assembly Hall into which they emerge at the sides of the dais. If the member ignores these three doorways (as he probably should) and proceeds along the corridor to his left he will come to a flight of steps, and if instead of climbing these he passes through a doorway on his right he will find himself in a passage-way with toilet and cloak-room accommodation on one side, and on the other a series of three doors giving access to the main Assembly Hall from the east side. If instead of going through the doorway he ascends the stairs, he will come to a corridor giving access to the East Gallery and finally leading out to the Lawnmarket. By turning right on entering the Black-and-White Corridor the member will have what is essentially the same experience except that for 'east' he must read 'west'.

The Common Room—This should be the goal of every member on arriving for the first time. To get there he turns right on entering the Black-and-White Corridor and then turns right again at the first flight of steps. He will find himself in a room set with a few tables and chairs and containing also a machine for dispensing tea, coffee, *etc*. An open-type stair leads to the mezzanine floor where the Clerks' Office is situated (see *p* 5). There is also a GPO Box and a stamp-machine and a board with up-to-the minute newspaper cuttings. Passing out of the Common Room by the other door the member is in the College premises, but he will also find near this doorway a public telephone.

The Rainy Hall—If instead of turning right out of the Black-and-White Corridor into the Common Room the member were to continue up the steps and straight ahead, he would find himself in the Rainy Hall. He would also most likely find himself in trouble, for a one-way-system operates here and he is expected to go through the Common Room and keep turning to his left until he reaches the Rainy Hall through a different door. In due course he will leave by the door at the head of the steps and so get back into the Black-and-White Corridor. It is important that he should make this circular tour, and this for two reasons: first, because in the course of his journey he will pass a *Cloakroom* where coats, *etc*, may be left under supervision (a consistently repeated story of lost garments necessitated the provision of this service and members are well advised to avail themselves of it); and second, because in the Rainy Hall there are to be found the *Ranks of Boxes* in which members may keep their papers and in which each day (from Tuesday on) will be found a copy of the Daily Papers (see *p* 28) and any other document officially circulated or at least authorised to be circulated. It is important to note that the number applying to the pigeon-hole is that appearing above it. The Rainy Hall also houses a book-stall run by the Publications Department.

The Area of the Assembly Hall—As has been noted, doors are to be found on every side giving access to the main area of the Hall itself. On most occasions membership cards have to be shown to gain admittance. Members may sit anywhere in the Area or in the West Gallery (there being no reserved seats) except that by long-standing custom the front bench on the Moderator's left is kept free for ex-Moderators, and the corresponding seats on the other side are kept free for the representatives of the Committee giving in its report at the time.

The West Gallery—The whole of this gallery (on the Moderator's right) is reserved for the use of Commissioners.

The East Gallery—This is a public gallery reserved for ticket-holders. Season tickets for the entire period of the Assembly and Day tickets for a particular sederunt may be purchased for a modest sum on application made in good time to the Office of the Principal Clerk at 121 George Street, Edinburgh.

The Public Gallery—The South Gallery is open free to the public and is entered from the Lawnmarket where on the occasion of a debate which has attracted wide interest a queue may be seen forming.

The Moderator's Room—On the wall at the east end of the Black-and-White Corridor is a drinking fountain. Just before that there is a double-door (unmarked). The wall immediately inside this is decorated with photographs of past Moderators. A few steps lead to a door on your right and this belongs to the room set apart for the use of the Moderator. Here each day he entertains a small party (about a dozen) to lunch. Anyone wishing for any reason to see the Moderator should not go to this room but should approach one of his chaplains. And bearing in mind how much he has to do, the business should be really important.

The Officials' Room–If instead of turning into the Moderator's Room the member continues up the stairs (a lot of them) he will come to a room used by what have been called by some 'the circumtabular oligarchy' and by others 'the boys in the play-pen'–the Clerks, the Procurator, the Solicitor, the Convener and the Vice-Convener of the Business Committee. This is not an office, merely a lunch and retiring room.

Ex-Moderators' Room–Immediately on turning in from the Corridor to go to the Moderator's Room a narrow stair goes down on the left. This leads to a room set apart for the use of ex-Moderators where they may keep their robes, *etc*, in case of being called upon to take the chair.

Press Room–A room is set apart for the use of representatives of the media. This is situated high above the Hall and is reached from the Lawnmarket side of the building. In the Hall itself reporters sit in the front seats facing the Clerks' enclosure.

Closed-Circuit Television–A complete system of closed-circuit television now operates throughout the entire sittings of the court and monitor-screens in practically all of the offices and side-rooms enable members to keep track of what is afoot at any particular time. This, of course, is quite apart from the arrangements made by the BBC for televising parts of the proceedings for transmission on the national programme. In recent years quite a bit of time in the forenoons is given over to live transmission.

First Aid–A professional first aid team staffed by members of the Red Cross is constantly on duty and when necessary the services of a doctor are normally available. The Red Cross team is to be found by going through the door to the left of that which leads from the Black-and-White Corridor to the Lord High Commissioner's Gallery, and turning left instead of passing through into the main Hall.

For the Hard of Hearing–Special, and I understand extremely effective, arrangements are in operation for the hard of hearing. Full particulars may be obtained from any of the Stewards.

Eating Arrangements–In the days when the facilities for lunch consisted of a number of tea-rooms stretching along distant Princes Street, a system was set up for catering in the halls of the Tolbooth Church. Today there is a wide variety of possibilities ranging from the humble snack to the slap-up lunch available within fairly easy reach of the Lawnmarket. There are also self-service catering facilities provided in the Hall of the Boys' Brigade in Victoria Terrace just across the way from the Lawnmarket entrance to the Assembly.

Parking Facilities–These present a very great problem indeed–parking is never easy in any part of Edinburgh at any time. On the Monday, which is a public holiday, meters are not in operation and you may therefore avail yourself of meter-space without cost–if you can find it. The Tuesday is also a public holiday (to the extent at least that the Post Office is closed) but for some reason meters are in operation and wardens are in attendance. Long-stay parking is available in Castle Terrace and in the former

Princes Street Station (enter from Lothian Road) but this is expensive–very much so. Many commissioners find it best to leave their cars in the suburbs and finish their journey by bus. Others find it best to leave their cars at home!

To Stay Over or to Travel?–Occasionally I have been asked for advice by someone whose home is within fifty miles of Edinburgh as to whether it is not as simple and convenient to travel each day rather than to find accommodation in the capital. I have always advised emphatically in favour of staying if this is at all possible. To come through in the train each day from, say Glasgow, means a fairly early start in the morning (*ie* leaving home at 7.30) and unless you are going to cut out the evening sederunt you will not be home until rather late at night (9.30 hopefully). And while sitting listening to speakers may not be an energetic way of spending your time, it can be a very exhausting way. Your day, therefore, has been both long and heavy. And when this is repeated the next day, and the next . . . ! The unanimous testimony of those who have tried both methods is that there is a great deal to be said in favour of staying over.

2

Preparing for Business

Having by now, perhaps, familiarised the new member with the sheer physical surroundings and the personalities involved, it may be appropriate to say something about how the action proceeds, thinking in particular of two things, the daily routine and the papers that are so important for an understanding of what is afoot.

Day by Day

The Opening Exercises

Each sederunt of the Assembly opens with the entry of the Moderator followed by praise and prayer.

The Daily Procession – Before the devotions each morning there is a small piece of ceremonial. The Commissioners being gathered in the Hall, the Clerks and the Procurator process from the east door to their places at the table. Very shortly thereafter, the Officer having called 'Moderator!', the Assembly rise to their feet while the Moderator, preceded by the Officer and followed by one of his Chaplains, makes his way to the rostrum. Once there he ceremoniously bows, first to those in front, then to those on his right, and finally to those on his left. This, of course, is duly acknowledged by each section in turn.

Everyone then sits down for a moment or so to await the arrival of the Lord High Commissioner and his suite, when they rise once more. When the Queen's respresentative has entered the Throne Gallery and taken his place he bows thrice as did the Moderator, and this is likewise acknowledged. The Precentor then steps forward and the opening devotions proceed.

The Devotions – Each sederunt of the Assembly is opened with praise, the reading of the Word, and prayer. This part of the proceedings lies wholly within the discretion of the Moderator, the only restriction being that the praise is to be chosen from the Metrical Psalms or from the Paraphrases. The suggestion has from time to time been advanced that on occasion a hymn should be included, and even that the organ might be employed to lead the singing. The latter proposal has never won much support – the singing does not need any mechanical help – but there is some sympathy for the former. In 1975, however, the Assembly solemnly resolved against the introduction of hymns. The singing is led by the Precentor, the Clerks take it in turn to read the Scriptures (usually nowadays from the New English Bible, although there is no rule), and the Moderator leads in prayer.

The Stewards have strict injuction that during the devotions they must not allow anyone to enter the Hall.

Officially the court has been 'constituted with prayer' and the minute must record to this effect.

The First Day

The foregoing represents the standard daily procedure, but special features characterise the opening day, the Saturday. That morning the Assembly convene at 10.00 and, because of the lining-up of guards-of-honour and other such exercises in the Quadrangle, the entrance from the Mound is temporarily out of commission so that members have to find their way in from the Lawnmarket. (Incidentally, to get from there to the east end of the Black-and-White Corridor the member goes straight along a corridor and down a stair with a left-hand turn to it.) Members are well advised to be forward in very good time that morning otherwise they are certain to have difficulty in finding seats. Somewhere around 9.50am the first procession enters the Hall from the east door, and this consists of ex-Moderators in full Moderatorial dress and ranged in order of their seniority as Moderators. They occupy the chairs set around the perimeter of the Clerks' enclosure. A little later come the Clerks and the Procurator. Then, after the usual call by the Officer, the retiring Moderator enters, followed by both of his Chaplains.

The Throne Gallery–When the Lord High Commissioner takes his place in the Throne Gallery on this occasion, he is flanked on his right by the Lord Provost of Edinburgh and on his left by the Solicitor General for Scotland. Also in the front row is the Purse-Bearer and, usually, the Secretary of State for Scotland. Immediately to the rear of the Commissioner is his Domestic Chaplain (who conducts prayers every morning in the Palace and who usually is his own minister), and also the Dean of the Chapel Royal. A most colourful back-drop is provided by the Lord Lyon King of Arms with his College of Heralds (Albany, Islay, Marchmont and Rothesay) in all the splendour and brilliance of their tabards, and also the Hereditary Standard Bearers–Dundee with the Lion Rampant and Lauderdale with the Saltire (the St Andrew's Cross). In the block of seats to the Commissioner's left is his wife ('Her Grace') with her suite, and behind them the Chiefs in Scotland of the three Services with their ladies.

Moderator's Lady – The first row of seats on the left of the Throne Gallery as you look towards it is reserved for the wife and family and personal friends of the Moderator-Elect. The row behind that is occupied by the wife and family of the retiring Moderator. The Moderator's lady is waited on throughout the Assembly by the wives of the two Chaplains. She gives a Lunch Party for ladies most days in the Georgian House. Normally too she invites to sit at her side in the front row the wife of whichever Committee Convener is at the time giving in his report.

Local Government Representatives – Prior to 1975 it was customary for the front rows of seats on either side to be occupied by the Lord Provosts, Town Clerks and Baillies of the cities of Edinburgh, Glasgow, Aberdeen, Dundee and Perth, all in robes–and a very colourful sight they presented. Since regionalisation an invitation is extended to the Regions which are to be represented, and so the tradition survives but, for better or for worse, the colour has gone.

Election of Moderator – Immediately the opening devotions have been completed the Roll of Commissioners is laid on the table by the Clerk, and then the Moderator has an opportunity to comment briefly on his year of office before concluding by submitting to the Assembly a proposal for the appointment of his successor. This having been approved, the Clerks and the two senior ex-Moderators go out and lead in the new Moderator followed by his two Chaplains. He is welcomed, consecrated in prayer, and the Moderatorial ring is placed on his finger (the first finger of the left hand). He then takes his place on the rostrum and his predecessor stands down. As a matter of interest it might be recorded here that the custom has now become well established whereby the 'reigning' Moderator is designed as 'Right Reverend', his predecessors as 'Very

Reverend'. (The latter style is appropriate also for the Dean of the Chapel Royal and for the Principal of St Mary's College, St Andrews.)

The Queen's Commission – The Assembly now turn their attention to the business of receiving the Lord High Commissioner, and the first step in this is for him to present his credentials–in the form of a Commission bearing the great seal of Scotland. This formidable document is handed down to the Clerk by the Purse-Bearer. In it the Queen expresses her regret at being unable to be present in person and gives her Commissioner 'full power, commission and warrant to represent Our Sacred Person and Royal Authority and supply Our Presence and hold Our Place in the said ensuing General Assembly'. The Commission is read out by the Clerk who obtains authority to have it recorded, the Assembly standing throughout.

Her Majesty's Letter – A letter from the Queen addressed to the Assembly and couched in much less formal terms is then handed over by the Purse-Bearer and this too is read by the Clerk to a standing Assembly. Again authority is given for it to be recorded, and a little later in the proceedings a small committee is appointed to prepare a suitable answer. This is submitted for approval the following day, the Assembly retaining their seats while it is read.

Address by the Lord High Commissioner – Next the Commissioner addresses the Assembly. Since he is speaking as the official voice of Her Majesty the Assembly stand for his address, although it is usual for the speaker after a few opening sentences to invite the members to be seated. The Moderator acknowledges the speech of the Lord High Commissioner.

Suspension – A number of items of formal business are now transacted, occupying only a few minutes, and the

sederunt is suspended for fifteen minutes before resuming for the business proper.

Resumption – The said 'business proper' usually begins with the report of the Board of Practice and Procedure and deals with matters of considerable importance for the administration generally of the Church (*p* 43). The sederunt can be counted on to end in time for a rather belated lunch and certainly in plenty of time for the Garden Party at 3.30pm at Holyroodhouse (*p* 79).

Evening Sederunt – An Evening sederunt is convened on the Saturday at 6.30 and being a separate sederunt this is constituted in formal fashion. The distinction should be noted between the Assembly 'suspending their sitting', which is merely a temporary interruption of proceedings, and the Assembly 'adjourning' which marks the end of the sederunt and is characterised by the pronouncing of the Benediction. Invariably nowadays the Assembly suspend their sitting for an hour or so at about 1pm each day and if they are still in session at around 5.30 it is usual for a second suspension to be made (*p* 68).

The Sunday

There is only one session on Sunday and that begins at 6.30 in the evening. No formal business is transacted on this occasion. Instead an address is given by the Moderator who has just retired (usually on the condition of the Kirk as he has found it in the course of his year of travelling), and thereafter Delegates and Visitors from other Churches are welcomed by the Moderator and three of these (on a rotation basis) are invited briefly to address the court.

The Monday

Monday's business sederunt is preceded by a Celebration

of Holy Communion within the Assembly Hall itself. In days past the Lord's Supper was dispensed in St Giles' Cathedral, but this resulted in a scramble to get back and secure seats, and in any case we are more and more coming to the view that the Sacrament is fittingly celebrated wherever we happen to be at the time, and in spite of the obvious difficulties the system has worked well and is, I think, appreciated. The Moderator presides assisted by a group of elders chosen, naturally, from among the Commissioners. Any Commissioner who would particularly appreciate the opportunity to serve should at the time of his appointment inform the Clerk of the Presbytery concerned, who will pass the information to the Clerk of the Assembly.

After a short suspension the business of the day is taken up. Three rows of seats on the Moderator's left are reserved for the 'serving elders'.

Church and Nation Day

A special rule applies when the report of the Church and Nation Committee comes to be taken–maybe on the Wednesday. This is the report which more than any other seems to lead to extended debating, to the lodging of many counter-proposals and generally to the taking up of much Assembly time. An experiment has recently been tried and is now written into Standing Orders–that of the application of a 'guillotine' so that any part of the business not concluded within a time determined in advance is simply departed from.

The Friday Evening

The formal closing of the Assembly takes the form of a separate sederunt beginning with the usual excercises at 7.00

pm, when there is a full-dress parade of ex-Moderators.

The Obituary–The Assembly takes up the report of the Committee on Deceased Ministers. A list is read out of the names of all those ministers who have died since last Assembly, and the immediate past Moderator leads the court in prayer.

Acts Appointing the Commission and the Assembly–The Assembly now goes on to pass two Acts, the former giving power to the Board of Practice and Procedure to call the Commission of Assembly (see Notes, *p* 90) to meet at any time as may be required, and the latter appointing the time and place of the next Assembly. It should be noted that it is 'the next General Assembly' and not 'the next meeting of the General Assembly', for each Assembly is a thing by itself. While it is commonly enough said that, 'The General Assembly *in* 1985 did so-and-so', it is more strictly correct to say, 'the General Assembly *of* 1985 did so-and-so'.

Reception–The Assembly next proceed to a reception of retiring Missionaries and Chaplains and other Agents, and of persons newly appointed to posts within the Church at home and overseas. Ministers inducted to their first charges since last General Assembly are also on parade and are presented. A comprehensive list of these people is printed in the 'Order of Proceedings' sent out with the papers (*p* 26). All are thanked and welcomed by the Moderator.

Moderator's Address–The Moderator then briefly addresses the court.

Lord High Commissioner's Address–The Queen's Representative now makes a short speech which traditionally closes with the words, 'Right Reverend and Well Beloved, your labours are now at an end and I shall inform Her Majesty that, having concluded the business for which you were assembled, you have passed an Act appointing the next meeting of the General Assembly to be held at Edinburgh on the . . . day of May . . . ; and now, in the Queen's name, I bid you farewell'. (It is interesting that the Commissioner falls into the trap of 'next meeting'!)

A verse of the National Anthem is then sung.

Closing of the General Assembly – The Moderator and members of the General Assembly having bowed to His Grace, the Moderator then turns towards the Assembly and says, 'Right Reverend and Right Honourable, in the name of the Lord Jesus Christ, sole King and Head of the Church, I now dissolve this General Assembly and appoint the next General Assembly of the Church of Scotland to be held at Edinburgh upon the . . . day of May . . . '.

The Assembly is now at an end and Their Graces revert to being 'Mr and Mrs'. One final act of courtesy, however, remains. The members of Assembly proceed from the Hall to line the steps and the Quadrangle as the party from the Palace, escorted by officials of the Assembly, make their way to the cars which are waiting to take them back to Holyroodhouse.

And so the Annual Business Meeting of the Church of Scotland is over for another year.

Papers

By Post

About a fortnight before the opening of the Assembly each Commissioner receives by post a parcel containing a number of documents. These include:

'The Blue Book' – This is the volume of reports prepared for submission to the Assembly by the various Standing Committees (*p* 42) and by certain *ad hoc* Committees. Each Report is preceded by a 'Proposed Deliverance' in num-

bered paragraphs, each paragraph beginning with a verb and presupposing 'The General Assembly' as its subject. These paragraphs represent precisely what it is the Committee is asking the Assembly to approve and adopt. Each paragraph has at the end in parentheses a reference to the appropriate part of the Report which follows where the facts are set forth and the arguments developed at length in support of that particular paragraph. The Report as such is merely 'received' by the Assembly–and unless there is about it something quite outrageous or offensive this is certain to happen. It is however, not capable of being amended, and this sometimes leads to confusion in the Assembly when someone is annoyed with the terms of the Report, wants to see it altered, and tries to move accordingly. The situation is quite simply that the Report *is* what the Committee has agreed–it is their report, not the Assembly's–and so the Assembly cannot change it no matter how misguided they may think it to be. The Proposed Deliverance, on the other hand, is what the Committee hopes the Assembly will decide, and the Assembly are in no way bound to do that. In due course the numbered paragraphs will be put one by one, and each requires to be approved, amended, or rejected by the Assembly.

'Order of Proceedings' – This is a quite substantial booklet printed on white paper of octavo size and containing (a) the Roll of Commissioners arranged in Presbyteries; (b) the Standing Orders of the Assembly; (c) a proposed Order of Business for each day of the Assembly; (d) a list of names put forward for membership of certain Committees and as Tellers; (e) some Notices and Intimations; (f) a list of those to be presented on the Friday (*p* 24); and (g) a print of Overtures, Cases, Appeals and Petitions.

The Roll of Commissioners can prove of considerable value as well as of interest to the member. It enables him to identify speakers who are all supposed to begin by giving their name and their membership number. Further, should he wish to make contact with another commissioner a note may be left in the latter's box, the number of which will be found in the said Roll. The Standing Orders are of considerable importance for the smooth running of the Assembly, but they are not usually of consuming interest to Commissioners on their first attendance. It is most important to have this booklet always at hand for the sake of the Cases which will come up from time to time in the course of the Assembly, where the facts set forth in the print are of great significance.

Membership Card—A little coloured card displaying the Member's Number on the top right-hand corner and with (attached to it) about a score of slips of white paper numbered and perforated for tearing out, will be found in the parcel and should be preserved with the greatest care, and for three reasons: first, it has to be shown to the Steward at the door to gain admittance to the Assembly Hall; second, when there is doubt about the result of a vote and a count has to be taken (*p* 77) it is the *sine qua non* of voting; and third, when it comes to claiming expenses at the close of the Assembly the Treasurer's Assistant will insist on having sight of the card.

Expenses Claim Form—This should be completed as directed and in due course presented for settlement. On the last two days a portacabin belonging to one of the Banks makes its appearance in the Quadrangle and here the claim form is presented and the money paid out.

Through the Boxes

Reference has been made (*p* 13) to the ranks of boxes in

the Rainy Hall. Members may keep their papers there in the appropriate space when not required. Messages and mail are also delivered by way of the boxes and they should therefore be examined regularly. The following also are distributed through this medium:

'Daily Papers'—From Tuesday onwards there will each day be an issue of a booklet similar in make-up to the 'Order of Proceedings', of a different colour each day, and bearing the title 'Daily Paper' beneath the date of issue. This document begins with that day's agenda, preceded by the words of the opening item of praise, and followed by the minutes of the previous days' sederunts up to about two days previously. Then come Notices of Motion that have been given in to the Clerks' Office.

Supplementary Reports—It occasionally happens that for some reason part of a Committee Report has not been ready in time for inclusion in the Blue Book or for circulation along with the mailing of papers, and in such a case a Supplementary Report will be put out through the boxes.

Other Material—The Standing Orders make provision that material regarding meetings of bodies connected (and unconnected) with the Church may be distributed through the boxes, but only with the advance permission of the Board of Practice and Procedure or of the Business Committee. Such material is to be treated at its face value, for although it comes in this semi-official way it has no official backing whatever. Clearly anything offensive will not be allowed, but the Business Committee inclines to be generous, believing this use of the boxes to be less objectionable than for members to have papers thrust at them as they come in from the Mound–and this they have no power to control.

3

The Nature of the Business

It is well known that the General Assembly is the supreme court of the Church. What is not so clearly recognised is that the General Assembly is the supreme court in three quite separate and distinct senses: for the Assembly is itself three courts wrapped up in one. If you are properly to understand how the business is conducted it is essential to recognise that there are these three capacities or roles and to be clear which is the role in which the court is acting at any particular time–in more popular parlance, which of its three hats it is wearing.

Three Capacities

Legislation–In the first place the General Assembly is the supreme legislative authority in the Church–although this generalisation is subject to a certain reservation (see 'Barrier Act' hereunder). The Assembly and only the Assembly has power to pass laws that will be binding upon the whole Church, or to declare what the law of the Church is on any subject. When wearing this hat the Assembly might be said to correspond to Parliament.

Litigation–In the second place the Assembly is the

ultimate court of appeal in all matters of litigation. A 'case' may have begun in a Kirk Session, but it can in the end of the day reach the floor of the General Assembly. Once there, the case has come to the end of the road, for there is no higher court of the Church to which it can be appealed, and it is well established that it cannot be taken to the civil courts. When wearing this hat the Assembly may be compared to the House of Lords sitting as the final court of appeal.

Administration–And in the third place the Assembly is an executive body, carrying out for the Kirk those activities which cannot be operated at parish level. In discharging these reponsibilities the Assembly works through Committees, and in May each year these Committees give an account of their past activities and seek authority for new enterprises, new expenditure, the engagement of new personnel, *etc*. When wearing this hat the Assembly may be thought of as a kind of Scottish Office.

It will be helpful to describe briefly how the court operates in each of these distinct roles.

Legislation

In criminal affairs there are two kinds of law: there is the common law, the rules that have never been written down but that are universally accepted as binding; and there is statute law, the legislation which Parliament churns out with such devastating persistence. Likewise in the Church not all law is to be found in formal enactments. It is not without significance that our official guide-book, 'Cox', is not called 'The Law of the Church of Scotland' but 'Practice and Procedure in the Church of Scotland'–that is to say, it is an account of how in fact the Kirk carries out its business, how it has been doing it for centuries. As an instance of the kind of thing I have in mind, when the barrier against women entering the eldership was finally lifted in 1966 there was no Act that could be repealed or amended–the rule that confined the eldership to men was just invariable practice so long continued and so firmly established as to have acquired the full force and effect of law.

All new law today is the product of statutory enactment and in the Kirk it will take one of four forms: (a) Acts passed after having 'gone down under the Barrier Act'; (b) other Acts; (c) Regulations; and (d) Injunctions contained in Deliverances that have secured Assembly approval.

Barrier Act Legislation–The Barrier Act was a piece of legislation enacted in 1697 at a time when the Church was in danger of reaching panic decisions and of being pressurised into unwise courses. As a defence against such contingencies the Act provided that before the Assembly could pass any Act that was to be a 'binding rule and constitution to the Church', such Act should first be proposed and passed as an Overture and then sent to the Presbyteries for their opinion. It might then be passed by the following Assembly, but only if 'the more general opinion of the Church, thus had, agreed thereunto'.

What in practice this has been taken to mean is that any Act that has serious implications for the whole Church must go down as an Overture to the Presbyteries, which are asked to indicate whether they Approve or Disapprove, and only if more than half of the Presbyteries indicate Approval can the following Assembly convert the Overture into a standing law of the Church. It is not enough that there should be a majority among those making returns. For this purpose there are today 48 Presbyteries in the Church (Jerusalem being excluded). If only twenty of these make returns then although all twenty are in favour, the Assembly will be powerless to proceed.

There must be at least 25 returns in favour. It should also be noted that the power given to Presbyteries is no more than a power of veto–no matter how many Presbyteries vote in favour of an Overture, the next Assembly are not in consequence bound to convert it into an Act. It is interesting too that no allowance is made for the relative size of Presbyteries or for the state of the voting, with the result that a vote of 9 to 8 against in one Presbytery would effectively cancel out a vote of 200 to 2 in favour in another. Once the Overture has gone down it cannot be amended in any way, except that an alteration may be made in its wording by the Assembly if they see cause, so long as it in no way changes the substance, sense, or intention of the Overture.

An Act passed under Barrier Act procedure has to be the subject of identical treatment if subsequently it is to be repealed or amended.

Other Acts–The Assembly also pass Acts which are not designed to be 'binding rules and constitutions' in the above sense. They used to pass Acts about the sale of property and the disposal of proceeds, although a simplified procedure has now superseded the need for an Act in such cases; they pass Acts erecting Church Extension charges into Parishes *quoad sacra,* they pass Acts, which are properly administrative in character, about the re-alignment of the boundaries of Presbyteries, about Quinquennial Visitation of Congregations, and the like.

Legislation of this latter sort does not call for Barrier Act procedure and the appropriate Act is passed on a straight vote in the Assembly. Until repealed by a subsequent Assembly such Acts are completely binding upon all affected by them–that is to say, they are no less effective or binding as Acts for not having 'gone down' to Presbyteries.

Legislation of this kind is normally initiated by one or other of the Committees of the Church and the text of the proposed Act is generally to be found printed as an Appendix to the Committee's Report. No special procedure is followed when the matter is taken up in the Assembly–normally a paragraph in the Deliverance states that 'The General Assembly note the position and pass an Act accordingly as in Appendix X'. The framing of legislation is a highly specialised affair and Committees and others submitting reports that involve legislation are well advised to consult the Board of Practice and Procedure regarding the terms of any proposed Act.

Regulations – These have principally to do with administrative matters such as the running of the Aged and Infirm Ministers' Fund, the employment of Probationers, the establishment of Church Extension charges, the granting of endowment for stipend, the payment of travelling expenses, the fees for pulpit supply, and so on. They have the same force and effect as Acts, and indeed are often associated with Acts or passed by provision of some Act. They are presented to the Assembly usually in an Appendix to the Report of the Committee concerned, and they become operative, unless otherwise ordained, on the relevant deliverance of that Committee being approved.

Injunctions – Often the Assembly 'recommend' that courts or groups or individuals should do, or refrain from doing, some particular thing; sometimes they 'urge'; occasionally they 'strongly urge'; and there are times when they go so far as to 'instruct' or 'enjoin'. This last, of course, can apply only within the framework of the Church itself (we cannot enjoin the Prime Minister or the Trade Union Congress), and it represents a very serious step since any failure to comply on the part of the body or individual enjoined is nothing short of contumacy and carries with it the most solemn consequences. Two considerations ought to be in mind when an injunction is passed: first that the matter is of sufficient importance to merit this kind of obligation being imposed; and, second, that there is some hope that the Assembly will be able to enforce it. Otherwise the supreme court could find itself in an unhappy situation. Of late Assemblies have inclined to 'enjoin' less light-heartedly than was once the case.

Injunctions appear in the body of the Deliverances of the Committee which has a concern to see that the thing is done.

It should be noted that any of the above forms of legislation, while usually proceeding from some Committee, can be initiated by a court of the Church prosecuting an Overture on the matter. For particulars of this type of proceeding see the paragraph on *Overture* (*p* 56). Or indeed an individual by Petition can ask for an Act to be put on the Statute-book–a kind of Private Member's Bill. It has also to be said that bodies which are not connected with the Church may approach the General Assembly by Petition asking that a certain course of action be taken which involves the use of the Assembly's legislative powers (*p* 57).

Nobile Officium–In virtue of being the supreme court, the General Assembly enjoy (as does the Court of Session in the civil sphere) a unique power known as the *nobile officium*. This is in effect a power to supply law where none exists–for a situation can arise which is quite simply not covered by any legislation. It was said of this power, by Sir Randall Philip, that 'it is used to give an equitable remedy which the strict law would not give'. It cannot be used to alter existing law or to justify ignoring the existing law if that is found to be unacceptable. Only very rarely has recourse had to be made to it.

Litigation

The General Assembly is the supreme court of appeal. There are a very few matters where finality of judgment is specifically reserved to the lower courts, but in most matters the road to the Assembly is open to the disappointed litigant. This type of business reaches the Assembly in the form of a 'case' and the relevant papers will usually be found in the booklet 'Order of Proceedings', although they are occasionally the subject of a separate issue. In a few matters the General Assembly is the court of first instance, but most of the litigation with which it has to deal comes to it as a court of appeal.

The routes by which cases reach the Assembly are: (a) Appeal; (b) Dissent and Complaint; (c) Petition; and (d) Reference. The first two are differentiated only by name, and for convenience they may be treated together under the common title of 'Complaint'. The first three represent the dissatisfaction of some person or body with a decision reached in a lower court, while the last represents the unwillingness of the lower court to come to a decision.

Complaint–The procedure under Appeal and that which is under Dissent and Complaint are identical and, as indicated, it is proposed to deal with them as one; but although we may thus treat them as identical, it is important to understand the distinction between them, for this is more than a mere difference in nomenclature. Suppose in a certain Presbytery one of the ministers was charged with some offence and judgment was given against him. It is open to him to *appeal* to the next superior court, that is the Synod. Let it be that the same result is arrived at in the Synod (the Synod would 'affirm' the judgement of the Presbytery) he can still go on and up to the General Assembly. In each of these instances he is the *Appellant* and his instrument is called an *Appeal*.

Suppose on the other hand that things had gone differently at the Presbytery and the minister had been acquitted (the charges having been found Not Proven–*p* 89) and suppose a member of the Presbytery felt sufficiently strongly that this represented a miscarriage of justice, then that member could take the case to the Synod, but he would do so by what is called *Dissent and Complaint*. Let's go on now and make it a little more difficult by suggesting that the Synod upholds the Presbytery and our dissatisfied member of Presbytery is still unconvinced. It is open to him to go on to the Assembly, but this he must do by the action called *Appeal*.

Or again, if the Synod had 'recalled' the judgment of the Presbytery and come to a different finding it was open to the Presbytery to take the issue to the supreme court–in that case too by *Appeal*. A member of Synod who did not fall in with the 'recalling' could take the issue to the Assembly–by *Dissent and Complaint*.

All of this must, I am sure, sound distinctly confusing, if not positively stupid. But it's really terribly simple. The principle to remember is that the person at the bar goes to the next higher court by Appeal, the person on the bench goes by Dissent and Complaint. And, you see, our dissatisfied Presbyter and Synod member in the above examples were members of the judging court when the matter was there, but were at the bar when it went to the next higher court.

Today most cases brought to the Assembly by complaint have to do not with the conduct of ministers but with issues of readjustment. The rules that apply are, however, exactly the same no matter what might be the subject-matter.

In all cases of this kind there are two 'parties'–the individual or court complaining about the decision reached at some lower level, and the body responsible for reaching that decision. The former appears as the Appellant and the latter as the Respondent. The rules about the hearing are discussed elsewhere (*p* 58). It is sufficient here to make two points: (a) after they have been heard parties are 'removed' and it is for the Assembly to reach a decision on the merits of the case, this being done under the ordinary rules of debate, any member being at liberty to make a motion on the subject; and (b) while a Presbytery which is at the bar may be officially represented there by two, or perhaps three, people, the legal position is that the whole Presbytery is at the bar (and is obviously no longer on the bench) so that every member of that Presbytery is debarred from taking any part in the debate and from voting in the division. This point is of particular importance when it is a Synod that is at the bar, since all its members are affected and it may well be that there are Commissioners from Presbyteries within that Synod who do not realise this. In such circumstances it is wise that the Moderator should declare that all members from the Presbyteries of A, B, C and D are at the bar and can take no part in the case.

Once a decision has been reached parties are recalled and the judgment of the Assembly is intimated to them.

Petition–This represents a much more general way in which the Assembly may be approached, and, unlike complaint, it is not confined to cases. In this latter context it is open to parties to a case only if they have been prevented from following the regular course–that of appeal. For example, if in his absence from a meeting of Kirk Session to which he had not been cited, an elder is found guilty of some offence and disqualified, it would, clearly, be impossible for him to appeal because that must be done at the meeting, and he wasn't there to do it. It may well be that the fact of judgment being passed in his absence forms the burden of his complaint. He has still open to him the remedy of petition to the Presbytery, and in the document in which he states his case he ought to make clear the reason for his following that course in place of the more normal one. In cases of this kind (which are rare) the procedure is exactly as in complaint except that the Session or other court, whose activities are the subject of complaint, are not automatically at the bar, although justice would demand that they be called there.

The more ordinary use of petition is to institute business in the Assembly as the court of first instance: a minister of another denomination will petition to be accepted as a minister of the Church of Scotland; a minister who has resigned or been deprived of his status will petition to have it restored; or a Presbytery will petition for alteration of its bounds or for dissolution of a congregation. Outside bodies may also approach the Assembly by petition, it will always ask for something specific to be done–this is its 'crave'.

Reference–A lower court may feel that a matter before it is of considerable importance and has implications wider than the purely local ones immediately involved, and that in consequence it would be wise to pass the matter to a higher authority. In the old days when Kirk Sessions were much exercised over the business of discipline it was not unusual for the Session to refer a case to the Presbytery. And there have been times when Presbyteries have referred important issues for decision by the Assembly. The crucial point about reference is that the referring court should have been unable to reach a decision or at least have considered it wise that it should not make a decision. If its judgment seems clear it should go on and pass that judgment and leave the dissatisfied party to pursue the matter along the normal paths. In effect, the situation in an instance of reference is that a case comes to the supreme court after it has been heard by an inferior court but without that body having reached a judgment upon it. Procedure is therefore exactly as if the Assembly had been the court of first instance.

A case of reference brought some years ago by the Presbytery of Edinburgh raised a most interesting point. The issue before the Presbytery had to do with the authorisation of a minister of another denomination to dispense the Sacraments–a matter which is put within the discretion of Presbyteries whose judgment is declared to be final. After lengthy debate a vote was taken in the Presbytery and resulted in a dead heat. The Moderator, rather than exercise his casting vote on an issue of no little importance, proposed that the case be made the subject of reference to the Assembly, and this was agreed. When the reference came to the Assembly the Procurator's opinion was that since finality of judgment was specifically assigned to the Presbytery the reference was incompetent, and this view was accepted by the Assembly which accordingly dismissed the reference. My own view (for what it is worth) is that the Procurator was wrong in his advice. The finality-of-judgment provision would be effective to secure that a decision once taken could not be appealed or challenged in any other way, but would not seem to me to make it improper for the Presbytery to say, 'We do not want to exercise this power of final judgment in a situation so important and so delicately balanced and so we wish to pass the whole issue unjudged to the higher court'. In such a case there is no other way in which it can be brought to the Assembly. It seems a great pity if a provision designed to protect a Presbytery is to have the effect of imprisoning it. I think the Assembly was free to send this case back, but I do not think it was bound to do so.

A new use of reference has arisen in consequence of the terms of Section 6(b) of the Readjustment Act of 1984 which provides that where a difference of opinion between the Presbytery and the Assembly's Committee on a question of readjustment cannot be resolved, the Presbytery may decide to refer the matter to the General Assembly. This does not seem a true use of the instrument of reference which is designed for a situation where a court cannot, or feels it should not, make up its mind. Here the Presbytery has made up its mind and has done so both clearly and firmly. The trouble is that the other body whose concurrence is necessary for a decision to become effective is holding equally firmly to a different view. The Assembly are certainly the body which in such circumstances should decide, but since the Committee is the creature of the Assembly it would seem to me more appropriate that the Presbytery should come with a petition craving the Assembly to instruct their Committee to concur. This, as I see it, would get the affair running on well established lines, and would save us from some of the fankles into which this new procedure is bringing us.

Administration

The complaint is sometimes heard that ours is no longer a Presbyterian form of government–we have become a bureaucracy. It must be granted that there is some substance in the averment. The trouble is that the conciliar system of courts that we call Presbyterianism was devised for a national Church whose affairs were confined within parishes, each of which was more or less self-contained, and is not equipped to deal with the affairs of a Church which sees its duty as stretching to the utmost ends of the earth and that recognises responsibilities which are national and not parochial in extent.

There can be no possible denying that the Reformers did a remarkable job in securing that the ordinances of religion would be available for every soul in Scotland, and devising the machinery to secure that degree of cohesion and conformity which would guarantee a national as opposed to a congregational Church structure.

But as soon, for instance, as the Church envisaged a duty to send missionaries overseas a situation had been created which demanded action not at parish but at national level. Though the funds might come from the congregations, the organising had to be undertaken centrally. There are many such activities today in which the Kirk Session can play no part beyond that of collecting financial support. All of this work is relegated to Assembly Committees. It is worth keeping in mind that these bodies consist of the very same people who constitute the membership of the courts–albeit they are arranged in different patterns. It is when the lines of the Committees and those of the Courts cross that the possibilities of a clash can arise and we hear disgruntled talk about bureaucracy.

Since the Committees are the creatures of the Assembly they have to use the annual meeting of that body to report diligence and to take instruction. This they do through the medium of Reports printed in the Blue Book. These Reports begin–they used to end–with a Proposed Deliverance which is at once a summary of the Report and a conclusion or series of conclusions based upon it. It represents what the Assembly are asked to do in response to the various items reported: the Assembly may be asked to 'note', maybe to 'note with interest' or 'with concern' or 'with gratification' or what-have-you; or perhaps to 'approve' of what has been done or is being proposed; or to 'authorise' some step it is suggested should be taken; or, as explained above (*p* 32), to pass an Act or a series of Regulations.

Once a Report has been submitted to and received by the Assembly it cannot be altered or amended (*p* 26).

But what of those Committees, those bodies whose Reports run to so many pages of the Blue Book and whose business occupies so many hours of the Assembly's time–what are they, and what are they supposed to be doing? First of all let it be said that a comprehensive list of the Committees showing how their membership is made up will be found in the booklet 'Order of Proceedings' under Standing Orders Nos. 109 and 110. As to what they do, the following very inadequate account may prove helpful.

Committee Structure

The Committee structure of the Church has from time to time been subjected to critical review and changes have been effected with the purpose of increasing efficiency and restricting expense. The most recent of such revisions was undertaken following upon a report of the Committee of Forty in 1976. The new machinery did not finally become operative until as recently as 1984, the subject having been studied for quite some time and the final negotiating of the changes having been undertaken by the newly formed Assembly Council after 1981. The principle that was envisaged was one of a system of Boards embracing the various Committees, although it did not take long to discover that the Committees do not readily lend themselves to neat and tidy grouping. The final results are shortly set out hereunder.

Administration and Special Interests

The Committees grouped here are probably the most irregular of all: they do not cohere to form a Department in any ordinary sense, there is no common thread running through their business, they do not share a common staff, they do not report to the Assembly as a single bloc. They are, in a word, the odd men out–important Committees that flatly refuse to fit in anywhere else. So here they are in a Department which is not really a Department!

Board of Practice and Procedure–This used to be called the General Administration Committee and that title is fully descriptive of its function. Its role is largely advisory in character, but it has direct responsiblity for the care and maintenance of all Assembly property, for compiling and recording the general statistics of the Church, for securing that all Church records are in safe custody, for overseeing the sale by congregations of all surplus communion plate, for keeping a verbatim record of the Assembly's proceedings, and in general for attending to the interests of the Church in all matters not covered in the remit of any other Committee. From time to time the Moderator, confronted with some tricky situation, seeks the guidance of this body. It also carries responsibility for all the preliminary arrangements in connection with the Assembly, including the printing of the Blue Book and other papers. It is always the first Committee to present its Report to the Assembly. The Principal Clerk is Secretary of this Board, and its Convener is usually appointed Convener of the Business Committee as soon as the Assembly convenes.

The Assembly Council–The various Assembly Committees have always been exceedingly jealous of their autonomy–they have seen themselves as answerable to the Assembly and to no other body. As an inevitable outcome of this, collisions have occurred and difficulties have arisen, and in 1967 the Assembly agreed (after a heated debate and on the casting of vote of the Moderator) to the creation of a new body called the Advisory Board whose function it was generally to oversee and co-ordinate the work of all the Committees, and in particular to regulate the engagement of ministerial staff. Since a considerable part of the membership of the Board consisted of officials of the bodies it was to oversee, it is not surprising that it proved less effective than had been hoped. And so it was that in 1981 the Assembly Council emerged to take the place of the Advisory Board–also after a hard and bitter struggle. This body has the remit to oversee, and where deemed appropriate to suggest revision of, the Committee structure; to keep under constant review the size of the office staff; to co-ordinate policies of the Boards and to evaluate the progress of their work; as well as to advise the Assembly on all matters affecting these Boards and their work, including questions of priority in the field of expenditure. The Council employs a full-time Secretary who, so far, has been a layman.

The General Trustees–Strictly speaking this is not an Assembly Committee at all, being a statutory body appointed in terms of an Act of Parliament. The General Trustees were created in 1921 to meet the need for a body that would hold Church property. Each of the Committees over the years had accumulated considerable assets both heritable and moveable, and these were held in a variety of ways involving many groups of trustees. All this property was to be conveyed to the new body. Then when, in preparation for the Union of 1929, it was proposed that the Church should itself take over (principally from the heritors) the various assets in the way of buildings and land and standard charges that were held for its behoof, the existence of the General Trustees provided a ready-made answer to an obvious problem. As the years have passed, more and more of the Kirk's heritable property has come to be held by the General Trustees, and the responsibility for securing its maintenance is more and more coming to be seen as their affair. While trustees are appointed by the Assembly this is not, as with other Committees, on the recommendation of the Nomination Committee, nor do they, once appointed, retire after a fixed number of years. They are in fact a self-perpetuating body with a Chairman, a Vice-Chairman and a Secretary. Each year they report to the General Assembly which in terms of the Act have power to make by-laws and regulations, which they must observe, as well as to remove members and to appoint members either additional or to fill vacancies. Among other duties, they ingather all teind stipend and income from glebes and pay this over to the Maintenance of the Ministry Committee.

Church and Nation Committee–The function of this Committee has been defined in general terms as, 'to watch over developments of the national life in which moral and spiritual considerations specially arise and to consider what action the Church may from time to time be advised to take to further the highest interests of the people'. It would be difficult to conceive a wider remit. The work is carried on by a series of sub-committees: on International Interests, Economic Interests, Social Interests, Commonwealth Interests, Scottish Interests, Church Interests, and Mass Media. The Report of this Committee can usually be counted on to provide one of the debating highlights of the week.

Panel on Doctrine–This is a Committee which was set up in 1960 with a view to securing a greater degree of consistency in dealing with doctrinal issues. It was felt that what had been the practice, of appointing an *ad hoc* committee each time some matter arose which had doctrinal implications, could easily lead to contradictory positions being adopted. It was felt too that an ongoing body with an overall responsibility could and would pursue subjects which emerged in the course of study but which did not fall within the remit of a particular *ad hoc* committee.

Panel on Worship–This is a Committee which concerns itself with matters liturgical and which over the years has been responsible for the production of Ordinal and Service Books and occasional Orders of Service for special events. Oddly enough, the content of these has never been made the subject of Assembly approval.

Nomination Committee–Standing Orders require that the membership of all Committees should change from year to year (four years is the normal length of an appointment) and it is the business of the Nomination Committee to bring forward to the Assembly specific proposals for filling the vacant places. It should be noted that, as well as this Standing Committee on Nomination, the Assembly at their opening sederunt appoint a Selection Committee to which questions are remitted involving choice of personnel which arise in the course of the business–the appointment of an *ad hoc* committee to do this or that, for example.

Stewardship and Finance

Prior to 1983 when this Department was established, there had been (a) a General Finance Committee which attended to the ordinary running of the Church, its offices and its affairs, as well as paying the bills for those Committees which were not fund-raising; and (b) a Stewardship and Budget Committee which looked after the funding of what were once called the 'Schemes of the Church'–the spending Committees. The income for the former came from a specific charge upon Presbyteries, known as 'Assembly Dues', and went into what was called the 'General Purposes Fund', while the latter represented the free-will offerings of congregations which were specifically contributed for Schemes. The funding of the ministry, that is the payment of stipends and expenses of ministers and also the payment of retirement annuities to ministers, was the affair of the Church and Ministry Department and a quite separate affair. The two former functions have now been merged and laid upon the new Board who have also been given some responsibility in connection with ministry. The primary duty of the Board is to promote and encourage Christian stewardship, but it has also to prepare a co-ordinated budget for the costs of ministry (active and retired), for the Mission and Service Fund, and for the General Purposes Fund, and it has to secure the Assembly's approval of this. It has then to allocate the grand total thus approved among all the congregations of the Church. It is this Board which exercises control over the General Treasurer's Department, including the running of the Church Offices.

Associated with the Board, but reporting separately to the Assembly, are the Church of Scotland Trust which provides facilities for the investing of Church funds, and the Personnel Committee for Staff in the Church Offices whose function is apparent enough from its name.

Ministry and Mission

This Department was formed in 1984 by the fusion of what had been the Church and Ministry Department with the Home Board. The work of the new department is carried out under three groupings–(a) Personnel and Finance, (b) Forward Planning, and (c) Mission. There is a Board whose business it is to co-ordinate the work of the nine constituent Committees.

Maintenance of the Ministry–It is through the office of this Committee that today all ministers receive their stipends, these being remitted (subject to the usual deductions for

PAYE, National Insurance, Pension Fund, *etc*) in the form of a monthly payment into the minister's bank account. The Committee is responsible, in consultation with Presbyteries, for fixing what is the Appropriate Stipend for each charge, and for considering and approving Vacancy Schedules, and where appropriate issuing Revision Schedules. The Committee each year determines what is to be the amount of, and in due course pays, the Minimum Stipend. It is important to observe that it is the Committee which makes this determination–in due time the Assembly 'notes' that it has done so. Were they so minded the Assembly could no doubt 'regret' that the Committee had acted thus–but for that year the Minimum Stipend would stay determined. It has the duty of reaching decisions, with the full authority of the Assembly, regarding the teind stipend resources of the former *quoad omnia* parishes–although this is today a matter of little moment. It concerns itself with ministerial expenses. And it makes an *ex gratia* payment to the widow or next-of-kin of a minister at the time of his death.

Parish Assistance Committee–This Committee engages Field Staff–mainly Lay Missionaries and Deaconesses–to work in densely populated areas and in remote sparsely populated areas. It also employs Youth and Community Workers and promotes a scheme whereby student summer assistance is available for certain parishes in the Highlands where a large influx of holiday-makers is to be expected.

Unions and Readjustments Committee–This body is generally referred to by its friends (if it has any!) as the 'U and R Committee'; and it is probably one of the best known Committees of the Church. It is entrusted with the very difficult task of ensuring that the Church's position on the ground will be so realistically readjusted that a ministry consistently shrinking in size will be able to meet its needs.

This it seeks to do partly by securing through unions and linkings a reduction in the number of charges that have to be manned, and partly by instituting a better deployment of available man-power resources through the establishment of Community Ministries and other non-traditional forms of parish ministry.

National Church Extension Committee–Two factors have in recent times contributed to restrict the activities of this Committee–first that there is not today the massive population movement of the post-war years, and second that the cost of new buildings has risen to such alarming heights. The Committee, however, continues to operate, if on a reduced scale, and new work is still being put in hand.

Retirement Scheme Committee–This is the successor to the Aged and Infirm Ministers' Fund Committee and it includes also the Insured Pension Fund, the Supplementary Pension Fund, and the Contributors' Pension Fund. By order of the General Assembly all congregations today must contribute 20% of the current year's stipend for pension purposes. Today also small annuities are paid to widows and other dependents of deceased ministers.

Probationers and Transference and Admission of Ministers Committee–This Committee (which constantly pleads to be called the 'PTA Committee') is entrusted with the allocating of probationers as candidates in vacancies. It operates also a scheme for the transference of ministers desirous of a change of parish. It has too the duty of processing applications for admission to the Church of Scotland from ministers and probationers of other denominations, although these actually reach the Assembly in the form of petitions from the persons concerned. It organises an arrangement for Pulpit Supply. Under recent legislation it meets and confers with Presbytery Advisory Committees in Vacancies to suggest names of suitable candidates.

Evangelism Committee – As is implied by the name, the concern of this Committee is for the spread of the Gospel especially through channels other than the parish ministry: St Ninian's Centre at Crieff, the Glasgow Lodging House Mission, and the Compass Ski Club are random examples of the kind of activity involved.

Chaplaincies Committee – The chaplaincies embraced in the concern of this Committee are those to Industry, to Hospitals, to Universities, and to Prisons. It is this body which has to make the appointments of chaplains and through which they receive payment; but in choosing the people, it works in close co-operation with the Presbytery concerned.

Associated Committees – Committees which are not part of the Department but whose work is closely related to it are the Committee on Chaplains to H M Forces, the Advisory Committee on Artistic Matters, the Diaconate Committee, the Society, Religion and Technology Project, and the Iona Community Board. The titles are probably sufficiently descriptive of the remits. The Committee on Chaplains to the Forces is usually given an Order of the Day for an afternoon session for its report, when all available padres are on parade as well as a senior officer from the Forces. The other Committees usually report immediately after the business of the Department has been completed. The Iona Community Board is not an Assembly Committee but is an Assembly link with the quite independent Iona Community.

World Mission and Unity

The Board of World Mission and Unity, successor to the Overseas Council and the Inter-Church Relations Committee, began to function on 1 January 1984 and carries responsibility for promoting relations with other

Churches, for developing partnership in Mission, for making nominations of representatives to, and approving grants to, ecumenical bodies, and for encouraging ecumenical initiatives at home and abroad. The Board has Missionaries and Chaplains serving in Africa, Asia, the Carribean, Latin America, Israel, and in a number of European cities. It functions through committees on the following: Relations with Churches, Relations with Institutions, Relations with Ecumenical Bodies, Personnel, Local Involvement, Finance, and Executive.

Social Responsibility

This Department came into being in 1976 to unify the work of what had been three Committees: Social Service, Moral Welfare, and the Women's Committee on Social and Moral Welfare. Its purposes are broadly defined as (a) to secure in the Church informed opinion on contemporary social and ethical issues, (b) to encourage balanced judgments on these issues and to press these judgments at all levels of influence, and (c) to offer compassionate service through the varied activities which it operates, and to encourage and enable increasingly caring work at parish level. The Department operates Homes for Children, Hostels for Young People in Care, List D Schools (although the Government is phasing these out), Hostels for Epileptics, a Hostel for the Mentally Handicapped, and Rehabilitation Centres, as well as forty-two Homes for the Elderly.

Kirk Care Housing Association—This is a quite independent organisation although it works in close co-operation with the Board. The major part of its work lies in the area of erecting sheltered housing. Its affairs, naturally, are not subject to report at the General Assembly, although if they were so minded the Assembly could resolve to make representation to the Association on some matter of mutual concern.

Education

This Department fulfils its remit through a Board of Education which is responsible to the Assembly for the whole work of the Department, and it operates through five constituent committees along with three Servicing Committees and a Public Relations Group.

Education Committee–This Committee acts for the Church in all matters of education in schools, colleges and universities. It appoints representatives to the governing bodies of the Colleges of Education, and it also appoints to Regional/Island Education Committees persons interested in the promotion of religious education in schools.

Education for the Ministry Committee–This is the body entrusted with the task of recruiting, selecting and educating candidates for the Ministry and also for the Auxiliary Ministry (although in the latter case the recruiting is the affair of the Presbytery). It supervises the Probationary Period which candidates are required to serve at the end of their College course before becoming eligible for call to a parish. It is also responsible for organising In-Service courses for Ministers.

Board of Nomination to Church Chairs–Where an appointment falls to be made to a chair in the Faculty of Divinity of one of our Universities, a meeting is called of a Board composed of representatives of the University Court and of the General Assembly in equal numbers, and, in terms of the Universities (Scotland) Acts of 1932 and 1966, if this Board brings forward a nomination on the strength of two-thirds of its entire number that nomination will automatically be ratified by the University Court. When, a number of years ago, a not wholly acceptable appointment was intimated to the Assembly a difficult situation emerged. Nothing could be done about the appointment–the most the Assembly could have done would have been to pass a Vote of Censure or of 'No Confidence' on those who represented them on the Board.

Youth Education Committee–This Committee is responsible for the Christian education of, and provision for, young people up to the compulsory school leaving age of 16. It provides curricula and resource material for Sunday Schools and Bible Classes and it lays-on the services of Advisers in both of these sections.

Adult Education Committee–This Committee takes over from the above at the age of 16, its work including the running of St Colm's Education Centre and College which is primarily concerned with the training of men and women for the home and overseas mission of the Church. Readers also come under the superintendence of this Committee.

Communication

The Department of Communication was the new name given to the Department of Publicity and Publication in 1983. It has the remit *inter alia* 'to keep before the Church the need for effective communication both within the Church and to the world, . . . and to provide for the Church of Scotland a professional service of publicity, publishing, bookselling, and production of the monthly magazine *Life and Work*'. It functions through a Committee on Publicity and a Committee on Publications. The former is a service agency for the whole Church and is supported from central funds. The latter is a commercial enterprise which for all its activities depends wholly on its trading profit from publishing and bookselling.

Publicity Committee—This Committee operates (a) as a Press Office providing a news and information service for the media, (b) as a Publicity Office producing publicity literature, display material and exhibitions, (c) as an Audio-Visual Unit producing highly professional audio-visual aids of all kinds, and (d) as an Audio-Visual Centre holding a wide range of films, film-strips, and tape-slides.

Publications Committee—This Committee carries the responsibility for *Life and Work* and for the British edition of *The Upper Room*. It runs its own publishing house, The Saint Andrew Press. The Committee also has a chain of eight religious bookshops situated throughout Scotland.

4

Getting Down to Business

You would not for a moment dream, I am sure, of writing a letter to the Sheriff drawing his attention to the fact that you had suffered grievously in both body and estate as a result of someone's reckless driving and go on to hope that the Sheriff will see his way to having something done to ensure that you will be suitably compensated. For we all recognise that the Sheriff sits as a court and that there are styles and forms that have to be observed by those who would approach such a body. The same is true of all the courts of the Church, and particularly is it true of the General Assembly. There are those who see all this as stuffy, antiquated and cumbersome and who would have the whole thing 'simplified', reduced to a free-for-all. There are those on the other side who believe it is good to have rules, and that in the long run you get there more quickly–and more fairly–by observing them. In any case the rules are there, so let me tell you something about them.

Instruments of Approach

Matters may be brought to the attention of the Assembly

in a variety of ways and it is important to understand these various instruments of approach. They differ according to their subject-matter and according to the nature of the body making the approach. They are (a) Report, (b) Overture, (c) Petition, (d) Appeal, (e) Dissent and Complaint, and (f) Reference.

Report–This aspect has been fairly fully dealt with above (*pp* 26 and 41). It is appropriate at this point to add that not only Standing Committees, but all committees of whatever kind appointed by the Assembly all bring the results of their investigations and deliberations to the Assembly in the form of a Report and Proposed Deliverance. All reports must be available beforehand in print. There is a further requirement that when a report includes proposals involving new expenditure, two days' notice has to be given and there has to be submitted an estimate of the amount of the said expenditure. It is also required that where legislation is asked for in a report a draft of the required Act is to be appended–and it is wise that this should be 'vetted' by the Board of Practice and Procedure.

Overture–This is the instrument by which a court of the Church–or a group of not less then twelve Assembly Commissioners–may bring a matter before the Assembly. The object must be one of wider import than the private concerns of the court or individuals promoting it. It should not be a proposal affecting the work of an existing Committee; the proper way to deal with that being a simple motion on the Report of that Committee. The restriction has, of course, to be fairly liberally construed since the parties interested cannot be expected to know in advance exactly what ground a Committee will be covering in its report.

An Overture from a Presbytery will generally have been initiated there by an individual member, but unless the

Presbytery is prepared to adopt it the matter will go no further, and once it has been adopted by the Presbytery it becomes the concern of that court and is no longer the exclusive affair of the person who originally propounded it. It may well be, of course, that he will be selected to present it to the Assembly.

Unless time will not permit, an Overture has to pass through the Synod on its way to the Assembly. That court, however, is bound to transmit it to the Assembly and can do so *simpliciter*, or it can add a Note–either of commendation or of condemnation. The Synod can act on its own initiative in promoting an Overture to the Assembly, but not a Kirk Session. Were a Kirk Session anxious to instigate business in the supreme court it would have two courses open to it–either itself to approach the Assembly by Petition, or to petition the Presbytery asking that it proceed by way of Overture.

Overtures are printed in the booklet 'Order of Proceedings' and the Business Committee arranges suitable times for them to be taken–usually immediately following the report of the Committee whose remit is most closely concerned with the matter raised. Where more than one Overture deals with what is essentially the one subject, they will be 'grouped' by the Business Committee and only one speaker will be heard for the group.

It is quite in order for any twelve Assembly Commissioners to submit an Overture to the Assembly. Except that this will be printed (at the expense of the twelve) as a separate paper, it will be treated exactly as any other.

Petition–Apart from the special use of Petition as a means of bringing the judgment of a lower court under review (*p* 37) there is its more general use as a means of initiating in the Assembly as the court of first instance an item of business which is the particular concern of the petitioners: for example, a Church Extension charge petitions for full status, a Minister of another denomination petitions for admission as a Minister of the Church of Scotland, or a congregation petitions for permission to sell heritable property and to apply the proceeds. Petitions have also been received on more general topics from bodies which are not in a position to come by way of Overture. Such petitions have been received from the Scottish Housewives' Association, from the Grand Orange Lodge of Scotland, from 'Shelter', even from the Synod of the Free Presbyterian Church–in relation to subjects as diverse as the Common Market, the reception of a Roman Catholic Visitor, and housing conditions.

A Petition always asks that something specific should be done and this is set forth in a 'crave'. The form of the Petition may seem a little odd, but it follows a perfectly logical sequence. It begins, 'Unto the Venerable the General Assembly'. It then says, 'The Petition of... Humbly Sheweth...', and there follows a submission of the relevant facts set out in numbered paragraphs. It then proceeds to the crave: 'May it therefore please your Venerable Court to...'. And it adds respectfully, 'Or to do further or otherwise as in the premises may to your Venerable Court seem good', after which it concludes with the phrase, 'And your Petitioner will ever pray'. There follows the signature of the Petitioner.

If a Petition is asking that legislation should be passed, then a draft of the desired Act must be included.

Appeal: Dissent and Complaint: Reference–These have been fairly fully covered in the earlier section that referred to them (*pp* 36*ff*). It should be added that in none of these should there be a 'crave' as there would be in a petition–the nature of the remedy must be left wholly within the discretion of the Assembly.

Presenting the Material

The way in which the Assembly deal with their business is covered very comprehensively in Standing Orders, and reference should be made to these–Nos 81 to 108. For convenience the following brief summary is divided according to whether the court is dealing with (a) Reports, (b) Cases, (c) Overtures and References.

Reports–The Report of each Committee is presented by the Convener in a speech that is restricted to ten minutes. The whole matter is now before the Assembly and discussion takes place, including the putting of questions to the Convener. When a question is a straightforward one designed to clarify some point in the Report ('Does the figure quoted include the expenses as well as the salaries of the proposed team?') then it should be properly answered there and then. But if it is an argument ending with a mark of interrogation ('Does the Convener not agree it would be wiser to delay the appointment for six months until...?') then it will be treated as discussion and dealt with in the speech which closes the debate.

If the Convener is not a member of Assembly it is still in order for him to present the Report, answer questions, and close the debate, but he may not move its adoption–that will be done formally by one of the Clerks.

When the Moderator decides the Assembly are satisfied there has been enough discussion he invites the Convener to move the adoption of the Deliverance and this is seconded by one of the Clerks. The Assembly now move on to consider the Deliverance paragraph by paragraph. It is usual for the Moderator to say, 'We now take the Deliverance–Paragraph 1?' The question-mark is meant to indicate that this is said on a rising inflection, and it is followed by a pause to see if anyone has anything to contribute. In the case of No. 1 this is unusual since the first paragraph normally 'receives the Report and thanks the Committee'!

At this point it is in order for counter-motions, amendments, *etc*, to be moved on each or any of the paragraphs as they come along, and anyone at all is entitled so to move, although precedence will usually be given to anyone who has a Notice of Motion on the paper. It is also in order to speak to the content of any one of the paragraphs, either in criticism or in support, even although one is personally not making a motion on the matter. Movers of counter-motions and of amendments are given five minutes, the seconding to be formal (but you can get five minutes to speak in support so long as you have not seconded!). When all motions have been moved the Convener has the right of reply to the debate in a speech in which he may deal with any or all of the questions or counter-proposals, but into which he may not introduce any new material. After that speech the debate is firmly closed, and it remains only for the vote to be taken (*p* 75).

When the Report is that of one of the Boards which has a number of constituent Committees it is customary for it to be divided into Sections, each covering the province of one Committee, and so at this stage the Assembly takes a Section at a time, allows the Convener or other spokesman for the Committee whose Section is under discussion to reply to the questions, and disposes of that Section completely before moving on to the next. The Report on Church and Nation is likewise taken a Section at a time.

As well as adjusting the paragraphs which appear in the print, it is in order to introduce a completely new paragraph to deal with some aspect not already covered. Such a proposal takes the form of a motion, 'Add a new No. 6 in these terms, "..."'. As soon as this has been read out the Moderator asks the Convener whether he is prepared to accept it, and if he agrees the Assembly are asked whether they agree. If the Convener says 'No', then the proposer has the right to speak and the Convener has a right to reply.

Even after each paragraph of the Report has been disposed of, the matter is, strictly, not concluded–the Deliverance in its entirety has still to be put For or Against.

Cases–When the Assembly don their litigation hat the procedure becomes distinctly more complicated, and strict adherence to the rules becomes imperative. Proceedings open by parties being 'called', at which point they proceed to the 'bar'. This is a bench in the body of the Hall directly opposite the Moderator, equipped with a desk and a microphone. In the case of a Petition there is only the one person or group of people, but in any matter involving the review of a decision there will be at least two parties–appellant and respondent–and if the matter has been to the Synod on its way to the Assembly there may well be more than two. Essentially, however, the procedure is the same whether the contestants be many or few.

In the case of a Petition the first step is that the Assembly must resolve that it be received. If it were couched in highly discourteous terms, or if it were asking the Assembly to do something clearly beyond their power, then it would not be received. If, on the other hand, it is thought by someone to be incompetent the best course is to receive it, subject to the question of competence, and then to go on and dispose of that point first. In such a case the challenger has the duty to speak first since he carries the *onus probandi;* and the Petitioner has the right of reply, it being understood that at this stage he confines himself to the question of competence. If the challenge is upheld the petition will be dismissed on this ground. It could scarcely have been so dismissed if it had not been received in the first place!

If competence is not at issue or if the challenge has been successfully rebutted, the party is now afforded an opportunity of stating his case, or, where there are more than one, each party has an opportunity of stating his case, the appellant, of course, being taken before the respondent. After the latter has spoken, the appellant may reply to any new matter that has been raised. And if he himself at this stage introduces new matter the respondent has a come-back. Questions are then invited from the floor, and these may be directed to any of the parties. It should be noted though that questions must be asked through the Moderator and not fired directly at the bar. When there are no more questions, or when the Moderator judges there have been enough, 'parties are withdrawn'. Properly this should involve their leaving the Hall, but in practice (unless for some quite special reason) it means merely that they stay in their place but are reduced to the status of spectators, unable to take any part in what follows.

It is now for the Assembly to reach a judgment on the issue which the case has raised, and this is done following the usual rules of debate, the Moderator calling for motions and a vote being taken. The person moving the first motion has in this case no right of reply. Parties are then recalled and the decision intimated.

There are one or two special rules that apply in the hearing of cases. Time limits are not applicable. There must be neither applause nor expressions of disapproval during the hearing. No-one should vote who has not heard the whole pleadings, and in particular no-one should vote against one of the parties without having heard that party's case. Since no-one should have his mind made up until he has heard the pleadings it is obviously improper for any Notice of Motion to be given in beforehand. If it is resolved that a case is to be taken 'in private' (which rarely happens) then the utmost confidentiality must be observed.

Overtures and References – Neither of these has the effect of automatically sending to the bar the court promoting the Overture or advancing the Reference. In these circumstances the Overture will be introduced or the Reference stated by someone appointed by the Presbytery for the purpose. If he is a Commissioner then it will be done from his place on the floor, if he is not a member he will do it from the bar. The debate thereafter proceeds in the normal way except that when the Reference has to do with a case the Assembly may decide to hear at the bar those who had been parties at the referring court.

Mention has been made (*p* 40) of the new use of Reference, to bring to the Assembly a readjustment case where the Presbytery and the Assembly Committee have failed to reach agreement. In such a case neither side is at the bar, but the congregation which is the cause of the dispute is there. To me it seems contrary to justice that the parties to such an action (Presbytery and Assembly Committee), each of which comes to the case with its mind very clearly made up, should be at liberty to vote. As I see it, they would be much better at the bar where they could be questioned.

Judicial Commission Report – A word may be said at this stage about a type of 'case' which really is not a case of which examples have caused considerable confusion in recent Assemblies, and which looks like being a growing cause for concern–I refer to the situation where the Assembly has to deal with the Report of their Judicial Commission on a particular kind of Appeal which has been dealt with by that body. As to the constitution and duties of the Judicial Commission, reference should be made to the Note on *p* 91. The Act anent Congregations in an Unsatisfactory State gives power to a Presbytery if it is satisfied that a congregation is in an unsatisfactory state and that this is due wholly or substantially to defects or errors personal to the minister to sever the pastoral tie. The Act also provides that a minister so deprived of his office may appeal to the Judicial Commission of Assembly but not to the Assembly.

The Act anent the Judicial Commission in turn provides that when that body has completed its hearing of such an appeal a full minute is to be prepared showing the various Findings, and this is to be submitted to the next General Assembly. When so reported, members of Assembly are to have the opportunity to ask questions. The question is then to be put by the Moderator with regard to each of the Findings in turn, 'Do the General Assembly approve this Finding of the Judicial Commission, Yes or No?' and the Assembly, without debate, are to vote. If the decision is against the appellant an opportunity is then given for a plea in mitigation to be offered by him or by his counsel. The Assembly are then to resolve whether or not the severance of the pastoral tie is to stand.

The cases so far have proved exceedingly difficult. The Assembly not unnaturally suffer from a sense of frustration at seeming to be asked to judge, and at the same time being put in a position where it is impossible for them truly to do so–how could the Assembly without having heard a scrap of evidence challenge a Finding in fact of the Commission which spent hours hearing the evidence? The plea in mitigation inevitably discloses facts (an *ex parte* statement of facts, be it said) and this readily leads to an attempt to hold a re-hearing. A Moderator calm, clear-headed and firm is required for such cases.

5

Keeping the Business in Order

Before trying to describe the order of debate in the Assembly there are one or two miscellaneous topics on which a word of explanation may not come amiss.

General

'Come to the Microphone!' – Until comparatively recent times a member wishing to participate in the debate spoke from his place in the Hall. Today, unless his intervention is confined to a couple of words, he must make his way to one of the microphones, of which there are three, one at each of the desks and one at the bar. The reason for this is not simply that people have lost the art of making themselves audible, but that both the closed-circuit television and the deaf-aid systems depend upon the speaker using the microphone. Since time is lost while you wriggle to the end of your bench and then walk to the front, the custom has developed that if you wish to contribute to the debate, instead of staying in your place and trying to catch the Moderator's eye, you come forward to one of the microphones and take your place in what may well be a queue that is forming there.

'Identify Yourself!' – When finally you do reach the microphone the first thing is to identify yourself by giving your name and your number. It may be an offence to our dignity to suggest that we are not universally known throughout the Church, but we must just swallow our pride and declare our name and number loud and clear!

'Address the Moderator!' – The proper form of address for anyone taking part in the debate is simply 'Moderator'– certainly never 'Mr Moderator'! Of recent years, since the membership became bisexual, phrases have appeared, all of them obviously designed to bring the traditional 'Moderator, Fathers and Brethren' into conformity with the facts of contemporary life. There is really no call for this kind of ingenuity. When speaking in debate the member is supposed to be directing his remarks to the chair, even although he is happy that many others are overhearing his observations. It is unfortunate that the need to resort to the microphone usually results in the Moderator being completely out of his (or her) line of vision. It could be argued that that very fact makes it all the more important that he preface his remarks with the simple call of 'Moderator!', while courtesy demands that ere returning to his place he should turn and bow to the chair.

The Bell – You are now in full flow–what about finishing? Unless in special circumstances your speech will be confined to five minutes' duration and you are well advised to have this in mind at the beginning and not just at the end. If you have not concluded within the time allowed, a bell will ring at the Clerks' table and this means you still have a few moments–not minutes–in which to bring your remarks to a conclusion.

Quorum – The quorum of the General Assembly is 31 of whom at least 16 must be ministers. It is most unusual in modern times for the attendance to fall to anything like this kind of figure–I am sure it must be 30 or more years since a count has been taken. It is not the duty of the Moderator or of the Clerks to ensure that there is a quorum, but it is in order at any time for a member to draw the attention of the Moderator to the fact that there does not appear to be a quorum present, and a count has then to be taken. If this shows less than the required number then the sederunt has got to be suspended. Any business which had been transacted before the challenge would be upheld as regularly done, and it would not be in order to seek to have a decision set aside because you were now in a position to prove that there had not been a quorum present at the time when it was reached.

Standing Orders–The order of debate is, of course, governed by the Standing Orders, but it is always in order to move the suspension of these in whole or in part when dealing with a particular item of business. You might, for example, feel that one of the items in a Committee Report was of very great significance to the whole life of the Church, and that since it was a matter on which opinion was sharply divided it was essential that there be a full and unhampered debate. In such a case you could move that the Standing Orders covering time-limits for speeches be suspended. To be successful this would require a two-thirds majority of those voting. Standing Orders may, of course, be altered on a simple majority vote, but this can be done only as a result of Overture and after not less than one day's notice in the Daily Papers.

Order of the Day–The arranging of the order of business is rarely an easy affair because it is almost impossible to forecast how long each item will occupy in debate. Not infrequently a seemingly innocuous paragraph in a deliverance will trigger off a long and heated controversy, while conversely what might seem to be a highly contentious report may slip through without challenge. To ensure that the time-table will not be wholly meaningless it is common to fix a certain item as an Order of the Day for, say, 3.15pm. What this means is that when 3.15 arrives the Assembly will conclude the item on which they are engaged (they are allowed to over-run to the extent of thirty minutes) and will then take up the Order of the Day. It is important to note that when that item has been concluded the Assembly will return to take up the Agenda at the point at which it was interrupted and not at the item following the Order of the Day on the Agenda. On occasion, however, the Order of the Day is shown as embracing, say Nos. 8, 9 and 10, in which case, of course, all three are dealt with before returning to take up once more at the point of interruption.

When, as has been known to happen, the business gets very badly out of hand, the Business Convener may intervene to suggest that some item or items be held over to a later sederunt. If this is agreed the report of the Business Committee given in the following morning will indicate what alternative arrangement is proposed.

Lunch Break—In the past few years it has been the invariable practice to rise for an hour's lunch break as near as possible to 1pm. It used to be quite a common occurence to go straight on, if need be, with the business, but this was found to be unsettling for someone who had a special interest in some item and thus did not know whether to nip out for a snack or to wait on hopefully. In any case it was felt that with all the heat engendered by the television lights (not to mention the debate) it is in everyone's interest that the hall should be vacated for a spell. If the court is still in session around 5.30pm it is customary for a second suspension to be made, or at least suggested, for it may well be thought more convenient to press on and finish the agenda, it being felt that many will not return for what remains of the business. Not infrequently a vote is taken to determine whether to suspend or to carry straight on.

Point of Order–Any member may at any time in the course of a debate (often in the middle of a speech) interrupt with a Call to Order. This represents a challenge of the propriety of the proceedings from the point of view of competence or relevance or regularity–for example, if in course of his reply to the debate the Convener is introducing new material. It is quite common too when arrangements are being made for the taking of a vote for a Call to Order to be made by someone who is convinced that the Assembly are not proceeding according to the rules. Immediately a Point of Order is raised, the interrupted speaker must resume his seat and remain there until the point has been resolved, except that, with the permission of the Moderator, he may explain why he believes himself to be in order. The settling of the Point of Order is the business of the Moderator who in doing so may, if he wishes, take advice from those at the table. He may even put the matter to a vote of the Assembly, but the responsibility for the decision still lies with him.

'Rising to a point of order' must be clearly distinguished from 'reaching a point of exasperation'. It is not unknown for someone to rise to a Point of Order on the ground that what the speaker is saying is factually inaccurate (although he may not express it in just these terms). Even if this claim is justified there is no ground for a Call to Order–the proper course in such circumstances is to join in the debate pointing out how far the former speaker has strayed from the path of strict veracity.

Dissent–It is open to a member on any occasion when a

matter has been finally decided to ask that his dissent be recorded. In the Assembly obviously this cannot mean the initiation of any process of appeal since there is no higher court to which to go; but the member may feel so strongly on the point that he wishes future generations to know that he at least had neither part nor lot in the decision. It is only when the matter has been finally disposed of that dissent may be recorded, and that is true even when the ground of dissent has to do with the procedure adopted at some earlier stage. It seems reasonable then that you should not dissent from a decision which had been unanimous–you should have taken steps to oppose it even if only to the extent of voting against it.

Other members are entitled to 'adhere to the dissent', and in that case their names will appear in the record. Only those who are present when the decision is reached may so dissent and you may not at any subsequent time ask to be recorded as adhering to a dissent.

Protestation–At the last sederunt of the Assembly, all other business having been disposed of, 'protestations' are called for. What that means is this: let it be that someone in a Presbytery had appealed to the Assembly against a decision of that Presbytery; then procedure in the matter would have been sisted pending the outcome of the appeal. Now suppose that the appellant does not withdraw his appeal but neither does he pursue it. In such a case the Presbytery 'protests' that its decision in the case has now become final and the Assembly grant an extract to this effect.

Guest Speakers–From time to time in the course of the proceedings space is found for a representative of such a body as, for example, the National Bible Society, to address the Assembly. While courtesy demands that distinguished visitors and representatives of closely affiliated societies be occasionally heard, pressure of business demands that such speeches be kept to a minimum, and the Business Committee tries to ensure that a fair balance is maintained.

Occasionally a Committee will wish to introduce someone who is not a member to speak in the course of their report. This has to be cleared in advance with the Business Committee which will usually insist that this speech takes the place of one that would have been made in the course of presenting the report.

Distinguished Visitor in the Throne Gallery–During his stay at Holyroodhouse, the Lord High Commissioner has many important people as his guests, and it is customary for them to accompany him to the Assembly. Advance notice of such visits is given to the Business Committee by the Purse-Bearer, and if the visitor is a person of national significance–the Prime Minister, the Archbishop of Canterbury, or the like–it is usual for the Business Convener early in the morning's proceedings to draw the attention of the Moderator to the fact that we have a distinguished visitor present and to say he is sure that the Assembly would be glad if he or she were to be welcomed and invited to address them. The visitor then comes down into the body of the Hall and after his or her speech is thanked by the Moderator.

Order of Debate

Debates in the General Assembly are conducted in a way that is well-established and effective and, once clearly understood, is seen to conform to some very sound and simple principles. It is at least as simple as any method for dealing with the complexity of debate on a multitude of subjects can possibly be. It is quite different from the methods generally followed in local government cirlces and various other bodies. To grasp it properly two things are essential–first an ability to identify the character of any proposal that may be the subject of a motion, and second an understanding of how the vote is taken among the competing proposals. It is, needless to say, an added advantage to understand why it is done in that particular way!

Character of Motions

Standing Orders define motions as falling into four classes: (a) the original motion, (b) counter-motions, (c) amendments, and (d) amendments to amendments.

The Original Motion–As the title implies this is the first proposal to have been moved in regard to a particular subject. In the case of a Committee Report it is the relevant paragraph of the deliverance that appears in the print. On any other subject nowadays there is no advantage in getting in with the first motion since, apart from the case of the Committee Convener, Standing Orders allow no right of reply.

Let's take a simple, silly example and follow it through the various stages and let's take it at Kirk Session level. Let's suppose someone moved at a Session meeting 'that a Session theatre-night, preceded by a dinner, should be arranged for the evening of 1 April'. This would be the original motion–much too original you might think!

Counter-Motions–The essential point to get in mind about a counter-motion is that it is a proposal contradictory to the original motion or to a substantial part of it. There may be as many of these as people care to think up. It should be noted, though, that what is sometimes called 'the direct negative' is not a counter-motion (still less is it an amendment) and that in fact there is no need for it to be moved at all. The person who wishes completely to negate the proposal (who in our example does not want any kind of social function at all) has his opportunity when it comes to voting For or Against it. And in every case without exception such an opportunity to vote For or Against must be given. This is not, of course, to say that the opponent is not entitled to speak against it, but in so doing he is not speaking in support of any motion.

Counter-motions are collected as the debate proceeds– that is to say, no vote is taken in relation to them until the whole discussion is closed and there have been brought before the court all the proposals that differ materially one from the other.

In our imaginery case examples of counter-motions would be, 'That a sail be organised for the second Saturday in July', and the second counter-motion, 'That a bowling tournament be held on a date in June'.

Amendments – These are defined in Standing Orders as being 'motions not substantially contradictory of the original motion, but for making deletions, alterations or additions thereto without defeating its main object'. That is to say, the amendment accepts the proposal contained in the motion or counter-motion but wishes to make a comparatively minor alteration to it by way of improvement. An *addendum* is properly a form of amendment, for it accepts the motion as far as it goes but wants it to go further. A deletion too will likely be an amendment unless it cuts at the very heart of the matter.

Examples of amendments in regard to our Kirk Session outing: 'Substitute 10 April for 1 April' in the case of the original motion; 'After "bowling tournament" add "for elders only, to be followed by a supper for elders and their wives"', in the case of the second counter-motion.

Amendments are disposed of one at a time on a straight

vote For or Against, and this may be done any time after they have been proposed and seconded. It is most important to note that the vote is For or Against the amendment and is not a vote between the amendment and the motion which it proposes to alter. In this way, you see, the court is avoiding reaching a final decision at this stage and is trying merely to get the major choices that are before it into their most acceptable form. It would, in fact, be more accurate to say that they are getting them into their least unacceptable form. You may well have to vote in favour of an amendment to the counter-motion although you are utterly hostile to the whole idea represented by the counter-motion, because if that is the way it is going to be, the amended form would be less objectionable than the original form. In our example, you may be all for the bowling match, may indeed have been the person who proposed it, but you still take your chance to vote between 1 and 10 April for the theatre-night, for at the end of the day you may find it is the theatre you are going to and it is wise to ensure that the date will be a suitable one.

As it has been said, the vote is For or Against the amendment. If the amendment were to be put against the motion then no matter which one was to carry, the matter would be closed, for the court had decided not merely that it preferred 1 – 10 April for a theatre-night but that it was having a theatre-night on 1 April. I remember many years ago presiding over a Congregational Board meeting about a vacancy when the stipend to be offered to the new minister was being discussed. I got a motion that the stipend be £700. This was followed by what I insisted was a counter-motion that the stipend be £800. One member with considerable experience in local government claimed that this was an amendment and demanded that I take a vote between the two. 'For,' he added, 'whichever of them carries I propose to go on and move a further amendment that it be £750'. 'O no, you won't,' I said, 'for whichever is victorious as between £700 and £800 represents a final decision about stipend and the matter will then be closed. Any subsequent motion such as you are now talking about I must rule out of order. So bring in your proposal now as a second counter-motion or remain forever silent.' I don't remember the outcome, but I do remember the ill-feeling!

Amendments to Amendments – As their name implies these are proposals to alter or adjust the terms of an amendment which is before the court. For instance it could be suggested that 'to be followed by a supper' be amended to read, 'to be preceded by a tea'. A suggestion of this kind is dealt with immediately by voting For or Against it and then putting the amendment–in its original or its adjusted form as the case may be–to a similar judgment For or Against.

Voting

Having in this way disposed of the minor choices, we have the main proposals before us in their most acceptable form and a decision has to be reached. In the case envisaged let us imagine we are now down to three possibilities: a theatre-night with supper on 1 April; a sail in June; or a bowling match preceded by tea in July–with, of course, the possibility still open that we resolve finally that we'll have nothing at all. So we put these to the vote–a choice of three for which everyone has one single vote. If the first count results 15:9:21 then none has a clear majority and so a second vote has to be taken, omitting this time the first counter-motion. We will thus have a straight choice between the theatre-night and the bowling match. If, however, the first count resulted 13:8:24 then the second counter-motion would be declared victorious since it had a clear majority–that is to say, even if all the sailors became theatre-goers the bowlers would still have it. No matter which one gains a clear majority over its competitors, it is still necessary that it be put to a straight vote For or Against.

I have heard it suggested that a short-cut could be effected by deciding in the first place whether or not we want a night-out, then deciding what form it should take, and finally getting down to the details. But this would not be fair. For until I know the precise nature of the alternatives I should not be asked to make an irrevocable choice in regard to them. As a person much addicted to sea-sickness I would not at all support the idea of a day-out if it were to be spent on the briny. As I have an engagement on 1 April I don't intend to approve of any sort of function fixed for that evening. By our way of voting we can exercise choice in this way; by the other, one would be accepting a pig which was, at least in part, still concealed in the folds of the poke.

You will often hear it said that you should always vote for the amendment first and that the original motion is always taken last in any count. To say that the amendment is taken first is true only in the restricted sense that you begin by getting the amendment out of the way, and this you do by voting For or Against it. It is not true to the extent that the motion and the counter-motions are put in the order in which they were proposed, and so inevitably the original or substantive motion is taken first.

Voting for Appointments–Where the vote is in connection with appointment to a vacant office within the Church and where there are three or more nominees, the method is the same as that between motions and counter-motions–each member has one vote, and counts continue to be taken until one name emerges with a clear majority of the votes cast.

Voting by Standing Up—When a vote has to be taken the Moderator will in normal circumstances invite members to stand in their places, first For and then Against, and he will decide which side has the majority. If he has any doubt, or if his ruling is challenged, then a vote has to be taken by papers.

Voting by Papers—Among the documents sent out to Commissioners (*p* 27) is a little booklet bearing the member's name in the right-hand corner and containing about a couple of dozen slips of plain paper, perforated and numbered. When a vote by papers is to be taken the first thing to happen is that there is a call for Tellers, and the Clerks arrange for every block of seats to be covered by one or more of these. The Moderator then intimates what number of paper is to be used. Those For the motion are then asked to stand and their papers are collected by the Teller for their block. The same will then be done for those Against. (It should be clear that no matter on which side you wish to vote it is the same number of paper you use.) The papers having been counted, the result of the vote is declared by the Moderator. It is quite in order at this point to challenge the count, and if this is allowed the whole of the voting-papers must be counted afresh.

Casting Vote—The Moderator has no deliberative vote but he has a casting vote, and in the event of the count revealing a dead heat it would be for him to decide the issue by using that casting vote. It is generally accepted (although it is not a binding rule) that the Moderator will cast his vote in favour of the status quo, the reason being that if a change is to be made–if, that is, we are to depart from the status quo–it should be because there is a clear majority in favour of so doing and it should not require the casting vote of the Moderator to constitute such a majority. Oddly enought I can think of only two occasions when the Moderator had to use his casting vote and one of those was responsible for the creation of a quite new Advisory Board (*p* 44).

In the other there was quite a difference of opinion as to what constituted the *status quo*! So the rule is neither binding nor simple!

6

Relaxing from the Business

Apart from lunches and suppers organised for special guests and overseas visitors, tea-parties arranged by year-clubs, and the various events of that sort inevitably connected with a gathering such as the Assembly, there are certain social events of general significance to which brief reference may be made.

The Garden Party

While officially it is no part of the business of the General Assembly, attendance at the Garden Party given in the grounds of the Palace of Holyroodhouse by the Lord High Commissioner is one of the events traditionally associated in the minds of most with the experience of being a Commissioner. Every Commissioner receives from the Palace an invitation for himself and a partner to attend this function which is held in the Palace Gardens and begins at 3.30 in the afternoon of the opening Saturday of the Assembly. For obvious reasons every attempt is made to ensure that the business will end as soon as possible after lunch-time that day (*p* 22). Along with the invitation comes information supplied by the Chief Constable about how to get there and what do do with your car when you arrive. While the rules about cars are strict and precise, there are these days no firm rules about the attire to be worn. Morning coats, top-hats, fancy waistcoats are still occasionally on view, and for most of the ladies the occasion is regarded as justifying the best from the wardrobe–although the ladies do well to remember that a snell wind can blow down from Salisbury Crags. Even if you forget your grey topper don't forget your Card of Admission or you will be in real trouble.

At 3.30pm precisely the National Anthem is played and the house-party appears through a french-window at the palace. They move out on to the grass and two large circles are formed by the High Constables of Edinburgh in their traditional blue uniforms and beaver hats and carrying their staves. In one circle the Lord High Commissioner, attended by the Purse-Bearer, receives guests, while his Lady, attended by her ladies-in-waiting, does the same in the other. The circles keep steadily moving away from one another until, around 4.30, they converge again and the party prepares to move indoors. Before doing so they stand in the doorway and the National Anthem is again played. In attendance in each circle there are one or two ex-Moderators and others whose duty it is to bring people forward for presentation. Should you wish to be presented, or should you have a friend say from overseas, the idea is to make contact with one of these 'presenters' who will then take charge of the affair.

At the end of the gardens on your left as you enter, there is a tea-tent where drinks, sandwiches, *etc*, are dispensed throughout the afternoon.

Palace Receptions

Receptions of one kind or another are held most evenings

at the Palace when the Lord High Commissioner extends hospitality to representative groups of people. Formal invitations to these events are sent out by the Purse-Bearer well in advance. Most days too His Grace has a small number of guests to lunch at the Palace.

The Ceremony of the Keys

On the evening of the pre-Assembly Friday a select company of guests is invited to dinner and to reside overnight at the Palace. A very much larger company is bidden to a reception thereafter when 'the Ceremony of the Keys' is performed. This is an act of traditional homage paid by the City of Ediburgh to the Sovereign–or in this case to the Lord High Commissioner as her representative. After a short expression of loyalty the Lord Provost hands over the keys of the city to the Lord High Commissioner who, having expressed his utmost confidence in the good faith and general competence, dependability and trustworthiness of the City Fathers, hands the keys back–with an air of relief. They would, I am sure, prove a considerable embarrassment–a police parking-pass would be so much more worth having than the keys of the city!

Moderator's Reception

The Moderator also holds a reception in the Signet Library in Parliament House (made available by the courtesy of the Writers to the Signet). This is held on the Wednesday evening and to it about 300 guests are invited. The Junior Chaplain is responsible for the arrangements and for sending out the invitations.

Notes

The following Notes expand considerably on some subjects dealt with (of necessity rather cursorily) in the course of the narrative of the earlier pages.

'The General Assembly Are...'

There is an accepted style whereby the General Assembly are always referred to in the plural–in the same way as the Crown affects the 'royal we'. Contrariwise, the lower courts must never be accorded this dignity. Thus while 'the Kirk Session *is*' and 'the Presbytery *is*', and 'the Synod *is*', 'the General Assembly *are*'. It may on occasion lead to an awkward construction, but it is a style which has been accepted and largely followed throughout this little book.

The Moderator

There is generally (and to an alarming extent among the media) a good deal of misunderstanding regarding the status of the Moderator of the General Assembly. It is important to begin by appreciating the fact that he is Moderator of the General Assembly of the Church and not, as is so frequently heard, Moderator of the Church of Scotland. Every court of the Church from Kirk Session to General Assembly is presided over by a Moderator who is complete master of order but whose authority is wholly confined within the court at whose meetings he takes the chair and which begins and ends within the period encompassed between the constitution of the meeting and the pronouncing of the benediction. He is not a 'Church Leader' in the popular modern sense of that term, and he is certainly neither a spokesman nor a plenipotentiary of the Kirk.

It was during the last century that the suggestion was made (within the Free Church, I think) that after the Assembly had risen the Moderator might be encouraged to visit some of the more outlying areas of the Highlands and Islands where people were feeling a bit isolated and forgotten. By conveying to them the greetings of the Assembly he could remind them that they were an integral part of a national institution. As might have been expected this proved a great success and the following year was extended, and so on, until the custom has been established whereby in the months between Assemblies the Moderator visits about half-a-dozen Presbyteries as well as some of the Church's stations abroad, and carries through a wide and varied programme of engagements in many parts of Scotland and farther afield. In all his travels he goes carrying greetings–and that is all he carries.

His Duties–From time to time questions have been asked regarding the nature and extent of the duties of the Moderator. In 1962, on the Report of a Special Committee, the Assembly agreed that 'the Office, Function and Duties of the Moderator are as follows: (a) to preside over the General Assembly and to perform those duties as stated in the Standing Orders; (b) to visit Presbyteries according to the scheme of visitation sanctioned by the General Assembly; (c) to perform such duties as may be directed by the General Assembly, and to represent the Church of Scotland on historic and national occasions as they may arise; (d) to undertake such other duties as he may choose during his term of office'.

In 1979 the situation was looked at afresh by the Special Committee whose remit was primarily to consider the method of appointment of Moderators. This accepted the 1962 proposition as adequate but pointed out in effect that Paragraph (d) provides a fairly complete carte-blanche. In particular the Report pointed out how the Moderator, once the media have got their hands on him, can be coaxed into expressing views which are purely personal views (and to which he is perfectly entitled) but which are liable to be taken up at the listening end as *ex cathedra* pronouncements; and also how Moderators have on occasion 'become involved in areas of public interest in ways which have not been authorised by the General Assembly and which would either have been disapproved by that body or would at least have aroused controversy if discussed there beforehand'.

These comments were noted, but nothing was resolved, so that officially the position is still as at 1962–including the wide remit of Paragraph (d). Ultimately, it has to be recognised, a great deal must be left to the good sense of the Moderator himself–and it is to be presumed that Moderators are chosen because they have a lot of good sense! And the crucial point to be borne in mind is that while the Moderator is authorised to undertake practically any duty he may think proper, he is not empowered to make either pronouncements or decisions in the name of the Church–only the Assembly can do that.

His Dress–A less serious but no less fruitful subject of discussion has been the formal dress worn by the Moderator. This consists of a cut-away coat with breeches, black stockings, court shoes with silver buckles, and lace ruffles worn at the wrist and over the left lapel. He also wears a signet ring. In 1981 a Committee looked into this question of dress (along with some others) and came to the conclusion that things should be left as they are. Two considerations principally seem to have been in mind–first that some form of distinctive dress, a unifrom of some kind, would almost certainly have to be found, and 'it would be a great pity to have to invent a uniform when we have one with a fair amount of history and tradition attaching to it'. And, second, that the testimony of ex-Moderators was unanimous 'that at home, and even more so abroad and when visiting the Services, immediate disappointment was expressed if for any reason the Moderator was not in full dress'. The Report also points out that there is no obligation in the matter and the Moderator is free to wear what he will.

On one point, however, the Report came out most emphatically, to wit that the wearing of the Moderatorial Ring should be retained. It would appear that the custom of the Moderator wearing an official ring began as recently as 1911. 'The wearing of a ring by the Moderator of the General Assembly may have been influenced by the custom in other Churches, but it is tied to no interpretation of any such custom; nor is any ranking or ecclesiastical status indicated by the fact that it is an amethyst stone rather than any other that is set in the ring.' The Assembly heartily concurred in the view that the ring should continue to be worn as formerly. It is solemnly placed on the finger of the new Moderator by his predecessor at the time of his installation (*p* 20).

His Coat-of-Arms–About a century ago it was common practice for printers to insert 'ornaments' at the beginning and end of chapters in a book. One enterprising printer produced for a Church book such an ornament in the form of a burning bush and the idea was thereafter taken up and perpetuated–in the way that these things are. So, in this quite accidental fashion the burning bush came to be accepted as the 'emblem' of the Church of Scotland. It appeared in different places in many different forms, and it was never officially adopted, much less registered as an armorial bearing. About twenty-five years ago the suggestion was made by the Lord Lyon King of Arms that the Church should register the burning bush. There was no reason why we should not carry on as we were doing, but as things stood any individual or society could adopt the symbol, register it, and then interdict its use by the Church. As a result of further consideration a standardised form was prepared and duly registered as the armorial bearings of the Church of Scotland.

A question immediately arose about the right of the Moderator to use the crest on official stationery, *etc*. It was pointed out that for this purpose a more elaborate affair was required to show in heraldic terms and devices the connection between the Kirk and the holder of the office of Moderator within it. So, with the help of the Lord Lyon, the present 'coat-of-arms' appeared. The Moderator has the right to use it only as long as he is Moderator, and he is not under any obligation to do so.

How chosen – In view of the countless commitments of the Moderator of today it is essential that he be given adequate warning so that he can make arrangements to be relieved from his parish, chair, or other normal occupation, as well as get down to some preliminary work on the many speeches he will have to make. So that although the Moderator is not elected until the opening of the Assembly–and the court have always been most insistent to keep this in their own hand–he is chosen by a Committee at a meeting on the third Tuesday of October. The Committee used to consist of all the ex-Moderators with an equal number of elders appointed by the Assembly, and two ministers and two elders appointed by each of the Synods. It came to be felt that this was too big (and too expensive) a Committee, and in some quarters it was thought that ex-Moderators were over-represented. Various changes were mooted, including a proposal that the selection should take place openly at the October Commission of Assembly (see Note *p* 90), and also that Presbyteries might officially submit nominations for the consideration of the Committee. The former suggestion gained little support. When it became apparent that the latter suggestion was leading to a degree of 'candidature' for the offiice it was resolved to depart from it.

A change, however, was made in the constitution of the Committee which now consists of the seven immediate past Moderators with an equal number of elders appointed by the Assembly and one representative (minister or elder) appointed by each Presbytery within Great Britain. The chair is taken by the earliest of the ex-Moderators willing to act, and the Principal Clerk fulfils the duties of Secretary.

The deliberations of the Committee are strictly confidential, but their *modus operandi* is well enough known–that nominations are called for and briefly spoken to and a vote is then taken, and if need be repeated, until one name emerges with a clear majority. It is customary to agree that this name be put forward as the unanimous choice of the Committee.

Process of Libel

The name 'libel' is that which is given in Church courts to the formal instrument by which a minister, probationer, or deaconess of the Church is indicted on a charge of misconduct or of heresy–the court concerned is said to 'proceed by libel'. The lowest court, obviously, in which a libel can be instituted is the Presbytery, but it is equally appropriate in Synod or General Assembly, although cases normally come there by way of appeal. It is very rarely in use today and I myself cannot remember a case coming to the Assembly, although I know of cases that have been heard within the Presbytery. What is at stake in such an action will usually be the status as a minister of the accused and the field is therefore one in which the court has to move with scrupulous care and the utmost impartiality.

How Begun–An action by libel is usually begun as a result of what is called a *fama*, that is to say, a wide-spread story that a minister has been guilty of some conduct unworthy of his calling, or has been spreading heretical doctrine. If the affair is so widely noised abroad that it has become a scandal–a *fama clamosa*–then the Presbytery must take action on its own initiative. If, on the other hand, the complaint comes from an individual, the Presbytery is forbidden from acting unless and until the complainer has submitted a subscribed writing or has given in his complaint orally in the presence of the court with a promise to make it good with sufficient evidence. Where heresy is alleged the issue will not likely be that of establishing what the minister said, but of determining how far what he may well admit to having said was in fact heretical.

Form of Libel–The form of libel that was originally employed within the Church is of considerable interest and significance. A charge of drunkeness would prior to 1889 (much abbreviated and simplified) have taken the form of a libel something like this:–'Mr AB, Minister at CD, you are indicted and accused at the instance of the Presbytery of X THAT ALBEIT by the word of God and the laws and discipline of the Church of Scotland, habitual drunkenness is an offence of a heinous nature severely punishable by the laws of the Church: YET TRUE IT IS AND OF VERITY that you, the said AB, are guilty of this offence insofar as on ...at...and on...at...: WHICH BEING PROVEN you, the said AB, ought to be punished according to the rules and discipline of the Church'. Here we have a perfect syllogism quite as straightforward as the text-book example, 'All men are mortal: Socrates is a man: therefore Socrates is mortal'. The major premise sets out the offence; the minor premise brings the accused within the scope of the subject; and the conclusion follows with inescapable logical precision. All that is outstanding is that the facts that are averred in the minor premise have to be proved–and that is what the trial is all about.

The duty of the prosecutor, then, is to prove the facts alleged in the minor premise, and the duty of the court is to determine whether or not he has properly discharged that responsibility–*ie* has the charge been brought home?

The Verdict–Some find it surprising that the verdict of acquittal in the courts of the Church is not, as in the criminal courts, one of 'Not Guilty' but is one of 'Not Proven'. But clearly in the circumstances outlined above if the court is satisfied that the onus of proof has been fully discharged they will return a verdict of 'Proven'; if not it will be a verdict of 'Not Proven'. In other words, it is not for the Assembly to decide whether or not Mr AB is an habitual drunkard–all that they have to decide is whether or not it has been proved that he is so. 'Guilty' and 'Not Guilty' are properly 'pleas' which the accused tenders at the begining of the trial, not verdicts which the court should pronounce at its end.

The form in which a libel is presented today has been considerably altered and simplified, but the principles remain unchanged and the choice of verdict is still the same. It should be particularly noted that a verdict of Not Proven is not to be confused with the so-called 'third verdict' open to Scottish juries in criminal courts.

The Commission of Assembly

From the very earliest of times the practice has been followed by the General Assembly of remitting matters to be disposed of by commissioners. 'With the single exception of legislation, there would appear to be no power belonging to the General Assembly which has not been exercised by Commissioners.' The only limits to the powers of a Commission are those delineated in the terms of the Act by which it is constituted–within these limits the Commission act as if they were the Assembly. They report to the ensuing Assembly what they have done, but they do not need to seek approval for, or ratification of, their actions.

Bearing in mind the comparative infrequency of meetings of the General Assembly it is expedient that there should be a body empowered to act in their stead between one May and the next, and this want has been supplied by what was called the Commission of Assembly–now simply 'the Commission'. This is a body appointed each year by an Act passed on the closing day of the Assembly (*p* 25). For many years now the Commission have consisted of the whole membership of the previous Assembly plus one other appointed by the Moderator and have met regularly twice a year in October and February as well as having power to meet at other times as need may arise. The business was often very scanty and formal, and enough ministers and elders to form a quorum from in and around Edinburgh met as the Commission and transacted the necessary items of business.

The year 1963 saw the introduction of the sytem whereby a payment is made towards the expenses incurred by commissioners attending the Assembly and also the Commission. This, predictably, produced a spectacular increase in the number attending the Commission! The expense–which was considerable–was thought to be out of proportion to the importance of the business often transacted; on some occasions it was obvious that considerable ingenuity had been required to compile an agenda, and even so the whole affair was over within an hour.

As a result in 1981 an Act was passed putting it within the discretion of the Board of Practice and Procedure to call the Commission as and when the need may arise, but continuing the right of a quorum (31, of whom at least 16 must be ministers) to requisition a meeting for some particular item of business if the Board is content that this is justified.

The principal powers delegated to the Commission are to dispose of any matter referred to them by the Assembly, and also to dispose of any matter affecting the general interests of the Church at home and abroad when the Church would be adversely affected by postponing consideration to the time of the next General Assembly.

The Judicial Commission

The General Assembly are the ultimate body to which an appeal can be taken in any process of litigation, but it must be apparent that they are a body ill-equipped to deal with an issue of any complexity. A court of 1300 judges is a bad start, and difficulties multiply when the issue is one that will take hours to hear. The Assembly are well able to determine the moral and spiritual principles that are at stake in any case, but it is not so easy for such a body to cope with the proof of the particular activities alleged in a charge. For instance, the Assembly can well discuss and consider how serious an offence drunkenness is in the life of a minister and what penalty it should incur; they are not so good when it comes to deciding whether Mr AB has been guilty of the offence. In the days when trials by libel had to be heard by the Assembly it was no uncommon thing for the court to sit into the wee sma' hours of the morning.

In 1940 an Act was passed which created an entirely new body to be known as the Judicial Commission, a body whose duty it would be to hear and determine appeals coming up from the lower courts in cases of trial by libel affecting the character and conduct of ministers (although not in a case of doctrine), but which would have no jurisdiction to propose, determine or pronounce sentences or penalties. In 1960 an amending Act was passed extending the remit of the Judicial Commission to include appeals arising under the Act anent Congregations in an Unsatisfactory State.

The Commission consists of 48 ministers and elders with a quroum of 24, although a hearing may not begin unless at least 30 are present. The chairman has a casting vote only. An appellant has a right to complain, on cause shown, against any member sitting on the Commission and if this is sustained the member is thereby disqualified. It is the remaining members of the Commission present who decide on such a complaint and their decision is not subject to review. Where an appeal has been taken only against sentence in the case of libel, or against the severing of the pastoral tie in the other case, it is to the Assembly direct and not to the Commission that the appellant must go.

The Commission enjoys all the powers of the Assembly

in the matter of citing witnesses, of examining on oath, of calling for the production of books and other documents, and the procedure generally is that which the General Assembly themselves would follow. The hearing goes on day after day until it is concluded. The minutes of the Commission are used to enumerate each count in the libel, or each step in the procedure of the Presbytery in the 'unsatisfactory state' case, and to show the Findings of the Commission in regard thereto; and this Minute is to be submitted in due course to the Assembly where questions may be asked, but where a decision has to be reached *without debate* on whether they approve each of the Findings, which are submitted *seriatim*. If the verdict is against the appellant, an opportunity will then be afforded whereby he or his agent may submit a plea in mitigation. The Assembly then proceed either to sentence or to decide whether the severance of the pastoral tie is to stand.

I am not aware of an appeal having been dealt with under libel, but one can see how difficulties would arise when the Assembly were asked to determine sentence in knowledge only of the offence or offences committed, and in ignorance (complete except for the plea in mitigation) of the circumstances surrounding the affair. Within the past few years an increasing number of cases have reached the Commission in connection with congregations in an unsatisfactory state. The trouble with these seems to arise from the fact that the whole idea of 'sentence' is inappropriate. No moral blame is attributed to the minister whose 'personal defects or errors' have been 'substantially responsible' for the unsatisfactory state of the congregation. The position in such a case is that although there has been no 'fault' of a culpable nature, it is thought to be in the best interests of both minister and congregation that their connection should be terminated, and accordingly the pastoral tie is dissolved. Once, then, it has been shown that the state of the congregation is unsatisfactory and that this is substantially due to the minister, the rest quite simply—and inevitably—follows, and a plea in mitigation is something of an irrelevance. Indeed one wonders whether the matter needs at that stage to have come to the Assembly at all.

Inspection of Minutes

There is an obligation laid upon all Courts and Committees of the Church to keep and securely to maintain records of their whole proceedings, and each court in its turn has the duty of seeing that this rule is being observed in the courts under its jurisdiction. Thus each Presbytery has an annual 'visitation of records' when the books of all its congregations have to be produced for inspection, and by the same token the Synod calls for the minutes of its Presbyteries to be produced annually. The General Assembly in turn call for the production of the records of Synods and of all Assembly Standing Committees. The booklet 'Order of Proceedings' contains particulars of the 'Committee of Synod Records and Minute Books of Standing Committees and Boards'. The books are divided out among small sub-committees for examination and report, and, before the Assembly closes, an omnibus report on the position is presented to the Assembly.

The Minutes of Assembly proceedings are printed in the Daily Papers from Tuesday onwards and are submitted for approval each morning at the opening of the day's sederunt. Clearly a backlog has built up by the time the Assembly close on the Friday, but this is taken care of when among the closing acts 'the minutes of sederunts not yet submitted are held as read and approved', and the Clerks are appointed 'a committee to revise the Minutes'. In this they are greatly assisted by the existence of the verbatim report (*p* 7).